MIX
Papier aus verantwortungsvollen Quellen
Paper from responsible sources
FSC® C105338

Uyi Benjamin Edegbe

Microfinance and Poverty Reduction in Nigeria

A Study of Selected Microfinance Institutions in Benin Metropolis South-South of Nigeria

Anchor Academic
Publishing

Edegbe, Uyi Benjamin: Microfinance and Poverty Reduction in Nigeria: A Study of Selected Microfinance Institutions in Benin Metropolis South-South of Nigeria. Hamburg, Anchor Academic Publishing 2013

Buch-ISBN: 978-3-95489-173-3
PDF-eBook-ISBN: 978-3-95489-673-8
Druck/Herstellung: Anchor Academic Publishing, Hamburg, 2013

Bibliografische Information der Deutschen Nationalbibliothek:
Die Deutsche Nationalbibliothek verzeichnet diese Publikation in der Deutschen Nationalbibliografie; detaillierte bibliografische Daten sind im Internet über http://dnb.d-nb.de abrufbar.

Bibliographical Information of the German National Library:
The German National Library lists this publication in the German National Bibliography. Detailed bibliographic data can be found at: http://dnb.d-nb.de

Dedication

This book is dedicated to God almighty and to the loving memory of my late Father, Mr. Simon Ekogiawe Edegbe who died on the 9th of December 1994. You were a loving and caring dad, continue to Rest in Peace.

Acknowledgements

First and foremost I want to thank almighty God for his grace and protection all through the period of this Study. I want to also thank Dr. Ernest Ugiagbe for his mentorship which increased my interest in carrying out this study. Also, sincere gratitude goes to Prof., Dr. Schwengel, Dr. Schumacher, and Pablo Nemina for taking their time to read through this work and offering very useful comments. This work would not have been possible without these useful comments and corrections to the draft.

I also acknowledge the support of managers and customers of the various microfinance banks visited for granting me audience during the fieldwork of this study. My appreciation also goes to Diplomica Publishing House for publishing this work.

I must not fail to thank my mother, my siblings and also the Idehen family especially Omorodion Idehen for all their concern, love, prayers and support throughout the period of this study. May the Good Lord bless you all. Special thanks to all my great friends especially Richard, Charity, Sampson, Jafe, Nnamdi, Steve, Marvin, Nosa and above all my mentor and big brother Dr. Ernest Ugiagbe for their support and encouragement.

Freiburg, Germany
August, 2013.

TABLE OF CONTENTS

List of Abbreviations

BLP	Better Life Program
CAC	Corporate Affairs Commission
CAMA	Company and Allied Matters Act
CBN	Central Bank of Nigeria
DFI	Development Finance Institutions
DFRRI	Directorate of Food, Roads and Rural Infrastructures
DMB	Deposit Money Banks
FEAP	Family Economic Advancement Program
FRN	Federal Republic of Nigeria
FSP	Family Support Program
GDP	Gross Domestic Product
IMF	International Monetary Fund
LGA	Local Government Area
MFB	Microfinance Bank
MFI	Microfinance Institution
NAPEP	National Poverty Eradication Program
NBS	National Bureau of Statistics
NDE	National Directorate of Employment
NDIC	National Deposit Insurance Corporation
NGO	Non Governmental Organization
PAPDC	Poverty Alleviation Program Development Committee
SAP	Structural Adjustment Program
SPSS	Statistical Package for the Social Science
UBE	Universal Basic Education
UN	United Nations
UNDP	United Nations Development Program
UNICEF	United Nations Children's Fund
WB	World Bank
WHO	World Health Organization

LISTS OF TABLES

Keywords: Poverty, Microfinance, Microfinance Institutions and Benin Metropolis

CHAPTER ONE

Introduction

1.1 Background to The Study

> *We will spare no effort to free our fellow men, women, and children from the abject and dehumanizing conditions of extreme poverty to which more than a billion of them are currently subjected.*
>
> -United Nations Millennium Declaration, September 2000

> *No society can surely be flourishing and happy of which by far the greater part of the numbers are poor and miserable*
>
> - Adam Smith, 1776.

The poverty question is a global phenomenon. It is perhaps one of the greatest challenges facing Mankind today, especially in most parts of the developing world. This Perhaps explains why the eradication of poverty was listed as the first of the eight issues of the millennium development goals. The problem of poverty is more disturbing giving the fact that there is abundant and enormous wealth in the world to adequately meet the needs of every one. Poverty may be defined as a condition of lack and inability to meet adequately the basic needs of life such as Shelter, food, education and health care. Similarly, according to a United Nations statement:

> *Poverty is a denial of choices and opportunities, a violation of human dignity. It means lack of basic capacity to participate effectively in society.*
>
> *It means not having enough to feed and clothe a family, not having a school or clinic to go to; not having the land on which to grow one's food or a job to earn one's living, not having access to credit. It means insecurity, powerlessness and exclusion of individuals, households and communities. It means susceptibility to violence, and it often implies living on marginal or fragile environments, without access to clean water or sanitation.(UN,2008 quoted in Ucha,2010).*

In other words, the problem of poverty is more worrisome in Sub-Saharan Africa with 47.5% of the people living on less than $1.25 and 70% living on less than $2 per day in Sub-Sahara Africa (World Bank, 2008).The figure may have become worse considering the drought that hit parts of horn of (East) Africa in 2011 and the problem of maladministration or poor governance bedeviling the region. In Nigeria the high level of corruption and poor leadership has contributed to exacerbate the problem of poverty. Ucha, 2010 puts it thus: "Unemployment, corruption, non diversification of the economy, income inequality, laziness and a poor educational system can be considered to be some of the key factors contributing to poverty in Nigeria"(p.46).

Given the fact that Nigeria is a country with rich human and natural resources, it is disturbing that majority of her citizens are still very poor. The government has over the years formulated a lot of programs and policies geared towards poverty reduction; however it remains a controversy whether those programs and policies have actually achieved their desired objectives.

1.2 Statement of the Problem

Similarly, existing literatures on poverty corroborates the fact that poverty is growing rather than abating in Nigeria. For instance, according to a recent data released by the national bureau of statistics (NBS), as at 2010, 69.0% of Nigerians (112 million people) were living in poverty an increase from 54.4% in 2004(see table 1.2.1).

Table 1.2.1 Poverty Incidence in Nigeria (1980-2010)

Year	Poverty Incidence (%)	Estimated Population (Million)	Population in Poverty (Million)
1980	27.2	65	17.1
1985	46.3	75	34.7
1992	42.7	91.5	39.2
1996	65.6	102.3	67.1
2004	54.4	126.3	68.7
2010	69.0	163	112.47

Source: National Bureau of Statistics(NBS)2012.

Also, the World Health Organization/United Nations Children's Fund Joint Monitoring Program in its 2012 progress report on drinking water and sanitation, ranked Nigeria third behind China and India on the list of countries with the largest population without access to improved drinking water. The report that covered the period from 1990 to 2010 added that 66million Nigerians lack access to pure drinking water 'while 34 million, about 20 per cent of the country's population practiced open defecation'(Okpi, 2012) .

In view of the following, the government of Nigeria has over the years especially after the promulgation of the Structural Adjustment Program (SAP) (a reform program aimed at restructuring and diversifying the economy initiated by the Babangida administration) in 1986 formulated a series of programs and policies towards ameliorating poverty. Some of these programs includes: Directorate of Food, Roads and Rural Infrastructures (DFRRI), National Directorate of Employment (NDE), Peoples Bank, National Poverty Eradication Program (NAPEP) and the Micro- credit/finance scheme. Of all the schemes stated above, the micro-finance scheme was vigorous pursued and promoted by the government as an instrument of poverty reduction through the delivery of specific and adequate credits to the poor to enable them fulfill their goals, reduce unemployment, and contribute to national development(Asemota,2010; FRN, 2001).

The micro-finance regulatory framework was first formulated in 2005 to replace all existing community banks and micro-finance institutions and mandating them to convert to micro-finance banks and was required to have a mandatory minimum capital of 20million Naira about $125,000 (CBN, 2005).

This research work is aim at exploring how well the micro-finance banks have contributed to poverty reduction in Nigeria. Specifically, focus will be on beneficiaries of micro-credits from selected MFB's in Benin metropolis and how it has impacted on their socio-economic advancement.

1.3 Objectives of the Study

The general objective of this study is to examine the impact of micro-finance on poverty reduction in Nigeria using selected micro-finance banks in Benin Metropolis as case study.

The specific objectives are as follows:

1. To find out the socio-economic and demographic characteristics of beneficiaries of microfinance loans in Benin Metropolis.
2. To examine the impact of micro-finance scheme on the living standard and wellbeing of the beneficiaries
3. Examine the possible constraints/ challenges faced by beneficiaries in accessing loans from MFB's
4. To find out the policy, regulatory and supervisory frameworks which guide micro-finance banks in Nigeria
5. Based on the findings of 1 to 4 above recommend policy objectives and other ways to improve the performance of micro-finance development in Nigeria.

Similarly, this study intends to answer the following research questions:

1. What are the socio-economic and demographic characteristics of micro-finance scheme beneficiaries in the study area?
2. What impact does micro-finance have on poverty reduction and wellbeing of the beneficiaries
3. What are the policies, regulatory and supervisory frameworks which guide micro-finance banks in Nigeria?
4. What are the constraints faced by beneficiaries of micro-finance scheme.

1.4 Definition of Key Concepts

Poverty: A condition of acute deprivation preventing a person from living a life of adequate wellbeing.

Microfinance: Microfinance is defined as the process whereby small loans and credits including other financial products are especially provided to the poor people in the society to enable them engage in micro business/enterprises and other profitable ventures.

Benin Metropolis: A metropolitan city comprising three Local government areas(Oredo, Egor and Ikpoba- Okha) located in the Edo State, South- South of Nigeria

Microfinance Institutions: Are specialized financial institutions set up for the purpose of providing loans to poor people and low income earners for the purpose of micro business.

1.5 Significance of the Study

There has been an intensive global awareness of the impact of microfinance on poverty reduction in recent years. This growing awareness results from the increasing level of global poverty and how it can be curtailed. The successes of the Gramaen Bank which was founded in 1976 in alleviating poverty in Bangladesh and the subsequent award of a Nobel Peace Prize on the bank and the founder, Mohamed Yunus in 2006 have drawn more attention on the usefulness of microfinance as an important anti poverty instrument. Not surprising, the world leaders in inaugurating the millennium development goal pinpoint microfinance as one important tool that would help in actualizing the first goal of halving poverty by 2015. Governments, international organizations and nongovernmental organizations (NGO's) alike have committed huge financial and human resources in microfinance institutions across especially the developing world towards actualizing this laudable goal.

A study of this nature which dwells on the importance of micro-finance scheme on poverty reduction no doubt will contribute immensely to growing literatures on microfinance and poverty. And the recommendations will be helpful to appropriate government agencies and institutions in fighting and reducing poverty in Nigeria and elsewhere. This study is structured into six chapters. Following this introduction are chapters two and three which discusses conceptual issues on poverty and microfinance respectively. Chapter four focus on the research methodology, while chapter five presents the analysis and interpretation of data. The recommendations and conclusion of the study is presented in chapter six.

CHAPTER TWO

Conceptual Issues in Poverty

2.1 Definition and Meaning of Poverty

Poverty is a symptom of an improper society; the people are the victims

-Mohammed Yunus, 2011

Perhaps, one of the most contentious and serious problems facing humanity today is that of poverty. Poverty may include an inability to meet ones physical needs and other kinds of deprivations ranging from people's lack of housing/ shelter, medical care, education including clothing and physical wellbeing, (Shillington et al, 2009; O'Boyle, 1991; Jitsuchon, 2001). Defining the concept of poverty in absolute terms is in fact difficult because there is no consensus measure or single meaning of poverty and defining who is poor (Rosenfield, 2010; Spicker, 1999; Akindola, 2009). However, some definitions are worth viewing.

According to O' Boyle (1991, p.1) "Poverty is a problem in unmet human physical needs. That is persons and families in poverty lack the goods and services needed to sustain and support life and the income to purchase the goods or services which would meet those needs". Weisfeld & Andrzejewski (2008) distinguished between two types of poverty; vis-à-vis income poverty and human poverty. According to them, income poverty is based on the understanding or defining of poverty in monetary income terms, this measure popularly used by the World Bank and the United Nations (UN) is regarded as the poverty line method. According to World Bank, this means that people living on less than $1.25 are in extreme poverty, while those living on less than $2 per day are in moderate poverty. In other words, human poverty includes material deprivation of people. This includes lack of basic needs of life like housing/ shelter, clothing, proper diet and other social deprivations such as "denial of employment, participation in social institutions and education" (Weisfeld & Andrzejewski 2008, p. 2). The World Bank 2000 explained poverty as follows;

> *Poverty is hunger, lack of shelter, being sick and not being able to see a doctor, not having access to school and not knowing how to read and write, not having a job, fear for the future, living one day at a*

time. Poverty is losing a child to illness brought about by unclean water. Poverty is powerlessness, lack of representation and freedom from servitude. Poverty is living in abject squalor and hopelessness (World Bank 2000, p. 52).

According to Townsend (2010, p. 99), poverty is defined by an inadequate resources of people which "fall seriously short of the resources commanded by the average individual or family in the community in which they live, whether that community is local, national or international one". For the World Health Organization (WHO):

Poverty is associated with the undermining of a range of key human attributes including health. The poor are exposed to greater personal and environmental health risks; they are not well nourished, have less information and are less able to access health care. They thus have a higher risk of illness and disability..., The poorest of the poor around the world have the worst health (WHO, 2012).

This definition explains succinctly the devastating health consequences and risks associated with poverty. In a similar vein, the United Nations (UN) defines poverty as "a condition characterized by severe deprivation of basic human needs including food, health, shelter, education, and information. It depends not only on income but also on access to services" (UN, 1999: 57; quoted in Spicker 1999, p. 232).

Furthermore, Spicker (1999), opined that poverty has different meanings 'linked through a series of resemblances', he identified 12 clusters of meanings to poverty. The first is that poverty is a 'material concept', which means that people are poor because they lack the basic needs of life like shelter, food, clothing and water. The second meaning is that poverty is a pattern of deprivation; by this he means that it is not just as a result of lack of needs but the 'pattern of deprivation' and duration of time in which the deprivation persists. The third meaning is that poverty is associated with limited resources; that is, the unavailability of adequate income and resources to meet ones 'essential needs'. This is particularly true of Nigeria because for instance, there are poor people that can barely afford to pay for transportation to the hospital even if they would get free medical care/service. The fourth definition or meaning according to Spicker is that poverty is as a result of one's economic circumstances caused by low disposable income. Similarly, the fifth meaning sees poverty as a result of low standard of living of individuals or families falling below acceptable standard or level. Inequality is the sixth meaning of poverty. According to Spicker, people are said to be poor because 'they are disadvantaged when compared to others in the society' who are living in wealth and opulence. The seventh meaning which is similar to the sixth is that poverty is defined in terms ones socio-economic class and position in the society. According to Spicker, the social stratification of the society placed some members in a higher position/class and others in lower position/class that have poor means of livelihood and have little or nothing to cater for their needs.

Similarly, dependency, lack of basic security and exclusion are the eighth, ninth and tenth meaning of poverty. The eleventh meaning is Lack of Entitlements; according to Spicker, people are poor and hungry not because there is no food, but because they cannot afford to buy the food that exists. The twelfth and last meaning of poverty according to Spicker is that it is a moral judgment. Piachaud, 1981 quoted in Spicker, 1999 puts it thus; "poverty consists not just of hardship but of unacceptable hardship..., it carries with it an implication and moral imperative that something should be done about it. Its definition is a value judgment and should be clearly seen to be so". The twelve clusters of meaning of poverty have to do more with the way the term is used by different people 'rather than with the elements of definitions' (Spicker 1999, p. 238).

Shillington, et al (2009, p. 2) defined poverty as "a human condition characterized by sustained or chronic deprivation of the resources, capabilities; choices, security and power necessary for the enjoyment of an adequate standard of living and other civil, cultural, economic; political and social rights". In summary, poverty is defined in this study as a condition of acute deprivation preventing a person from living a life of adequate wellbeing.

The following different definitions bring to fore the different perspectives and understanding of what the concept of poverty is all about. As a result, it will be germane to further espouse on the meaning of this concept of poverty by explaining four different approaches which are; Monetary Approach, Capability Approach, Social Exclusion Approach and Participatory Approach. These approaches serve as a clarification to the various definitions above and also provides an 'alternative understanding' of poverty or who is poor? (See Laderchi, Saith,& Stewart 2003).

Monetary Approach

The monetary approach to the understanding of poverty is mostly used by economics to define and measure poverty. This approach sees poverty as a phenomenon caused by lack of adequate monetary finance to meet the daily needs of life. It is popularly called the "Poverty Line" method.

The monetary approach originated from the famous works of Booth and Rowntree in their different studies of London and York in the late nineteenth and early twentieth century respectively. But Rowntree's work on the survey of York which was undertaken starting from 1899 is generally believed to be the first major scientific study of poverty. According to Laderchi (2006), this research work of Rowntree is "generally described as the first scientific study of poverty mostly because of the high level of sophistication he applied in deriving a modern poverty line and in particular in estimating the minimal food requirements for maintaining efficiency on the basis of recently calculated nutritional standards. Such minimal requirements, together with those necessary for the purchase of clothing and rent, were added up to identify a poverty line, so that households whose income level fell below it were deemed to be in primary poverty" (Laderchi 2006,p. 6).

The Monetary approach has always been used to define and explain poverty in Nigeria; the understanding and definitions by most writers in Nigeria are usually focused on deprivation, inadequacy, consumption and income (Ugiagbe, 2012). This concurs with Tella 1997 (quoted in Ugiagbe 2012, p. 16), "people are poverty stricken when their incomes even if adequate for survival, fall radically behind that of the community… They are degraded, for in the literal sense they live outside the grades or categories which the community regards as acceptable (standard of living)". Critics of the monetary approach believe that the definition of poverty around a single approach of monetary consideration is not sufficient. Laderchi (2000, pp. 3) puts it thus;"The main problem with the identification of the monetary approach as an analytical category is that different conceptual reconstructions might underlie similar practices, so that equating them with one homogeneous category is not only artificial but possibly misleading" Another problem with the monetary approach is that it focused too much on the 'material aspects' of poverty (income and consumption) and neglected the non material aspects which includes 'quality of life, quality health and educational attainment' (Odusola, 1997).

Capability Approach

The capability approach originated famously from the works of an India scholar and noble price winner for economics Amartya Sen. The capability approach differs from the monetary approach that focus specifically on real income, wealth and consumption as explanations of poverty. This approach is concerned with evaluating a person's 'actual ability to achieve various functioning's' as part of a daily living. (Sen 1993, p.30).

The main tenets of the capability approach is that people should have the capability and freedom to do what they are effectively able to do , and also to live the type of life they are capable of living(Sen 1993, 1983,1985;Robeyns 2005;Laderchi, Saith & Stewart 2003). Consequently, the approach sees poverty as the result of lack of capability by the poor to be able to achieve a state of 'adequate wellbeing'. This approach focused on some important functioning and the corresponding basic capabilities a person should have. Some of which includes; the ability to be well nourished, well sheltered and the 'capability of escaping avoidable morbidity and premature mortality' (Sen, 1993,p. 31).

According to Sen (1993), human capabilities are an important aspect of human freedom and that a person's capability depends on different factors which includes 'personal characteristics and social arrangement'. In relation to poverty for instance, factors like high level of inequality and the failure of some individuals to properly situate themselves in a good position in the society may affect their capability and freedom to live a better life. Similarly, he criticized the monetary approach and explained that the approach can be incorrect and 'misleading' in the 'identification and evaluation of poverty'. Hence he opined that the problem of establishing and measuring poverty can be resolved much easily if a minimum 'combination of basic capabilities are identified' and that this can produce a different result entirely compared to when monetary approach that focus on some certain income criteria is used (Sen 1993, p.40).

Social Exclusion Approach

The social exclusion approach originated from Western Europe in the 1970's. The approach was developed to explain the level of deprivation and marginalization that existed in wealthy nations that had good welfare provisions for the poor in the society. The term social exclusion was first used in 1974 by Rene Lenoir, a French sociologist and the then French secretary of state for social action in government. He used the term to describe people who did not fit into the principles and norms of the industrial societies that were excluded from social insurance and tagged as 'social misfits'. The people that fall into this category according to him includes; the handicapped, drug users, delinquents and the aged. (Laderchi, Saith & Stewart 2003,p. 20).

According to the European Union, Social Exclusion is defined as a 'process through which individuals or groups are wholly or partially excluded from full participation in the society in which they live' (European Foundation 1995, quoted in Laderchi, Saith & Stewart 2003, p.20). This definition 'echoes' the work of Townsend. For him, 'poverty is not an absolute state, it is relative deprivation' (Townsend 2010, p. 99). He explained that people in the society are rich or poor depending on the share of the societal resources that is available to them.

The social exclusion approach with its focus on deprivation and marginalization adequately explains the poverty situation in Nigeria which affects more women and children. For instance, the 2007 UNICEF situational assessment and analysis of poverty in Nigeria lays credence to the fact of social and economic discrimination against women and children. According to the report, women and children make up 77 percent of the total population of people in poverty. The report also added that the estimated population of children in poverty is far greater than the combined population of both men and women in poverty. This is pointer to the fact that the rights of both women and children are still being greatly violated and consequently remain socially excluded and marginalized in the general societal arrangements in Nigeria.

The major difference between this theory and the previous ones (Monetary and Capabilities) is that the social exclusion approach focus more on the structural characteristics and more specifically on the marginalization of the (poor) socially excluded people in the society. The two previous approaches failed to lay emphasis on the socio-political and economic arrangements that contribute to deprive the poor people in the society access to basic needs that are 'fundamental to their overall wellbeing'(Ugiagbe 2012). Laderchi, Saith & Stewart concurs to this. They put it thus; "Social Exclusion is socially defined, and is often a characteristics of groups – the aged, handicapped, racial or ethnic categories - rather than pertaining to individuals" (Laderchi, Saith & Stewart 2003, p. 21).

Participatory Approach

The participatory approach to the understanding of poverty emerged from the Participatory Rural Appraisal (PRA) research work pioneered by Robert Chambers in 1994. This approach is a great departure from the three approaches explained above. It criticized the other approaches and noted that it was imposed from outside without seeking the views of the poor themselves. The main focus of this approach is to change this pattern of imposition and get the poor involved by seeking their views in ascertaining the true meaning of poverty and the problems associated with being poor and also having a say in ameliorating their plight (Chambers 1994; 1997).

According to Chambers, the PRA have 'three prescriptive ideas' which are as follows: First is that poor people are creative and capable, they can and should do much of their own investigation, analysis and planning. Secondly, that outsider has roles as conveners, catalysts and facilitators. Lastly, that the weak and marginalized can and should be empowered (Chambers 1994, p. 954).

Similarly, for any poverty reduction strategy to work successfully it must address the problems and needs identified by the poor themselves. This is necessary because their involvement and participation in promulgating and implementing poverty reduction strategies largely makes it possible for their knowledge to be used. Hence "participation is deemed to be the life-blood of contemporary poverty alleviation and rural development efforts" (Chisinga 2003, p.131-132).
One major concern or problem about the participatory approach is that the poor most times are shy to talk about their plight to other people. Field work experiences have proved this assertion right. Most poor people do not really tell the true state of their situation, they rather prefer to be quiet (Dodson & Schmalzbauer, 2005). As Scott 1990 puts it;"people confined to social margins maybe reluctant to tell what they know because they understand doing so as giving information to the enemy" (Quoted in Dodson & Schmalzbauer 2005, p. 950).
In sum, the following according to Maxwell (2009, p.1) summarizes how poverty is being generally described by different authors and approaches; Income or consumption poverty, Human (under)development, Social exclusion, Ill-being, (Lack of) capability and functioning, Vulnerability, Livelihood un-sustainability, Lack of basic needs and Relative deprivation.

2.2 Measurement of Poverty

The concept of poverty is very complex. Hence, the measurement is very crucial to determining the kind of method or 'intervention strategies' to be adopted in reducing poverty. Maxwell (2009) posits that "measuring poverty is not the same as understanding why it occurs" (p.1).

As explained earlier, 'Modern scientific' measurement of poverty emanates from the 19th and early 20th century works of Charles Booth and Seebohm Rowntree in their different studies of London and York respectively (Ringen, 2009; Laderchi, C. R. 2000; Laderchi, Saith,& Stewart 2003). According to Coudouel, Hentschel, & Wodon, (2002) measuring poverty requires three major 'ingredients'. The first is to 'choose the relevant dimension and indicator of wellbeing'. The second is to choose a 'poverty line' and lastly to 'select a poverty measure to be used for reporting' for the entire population (p. 30).

Firstly, wellbeing includes monetary and non monetary dimensions. The monetary dimension which according to them is quantitative includes income and consumption. While income have to do with the amount of money available to an individual or household when compared with other members of the society, consumption reflects the goods and services an individual or household 'command' or consume based on available income. The non monetary dimension measures other aspects of individual and family wellbeing 'like health, nutrition, and literacy and with deficient social relations; insecurity, low self esteem and powerlessness (Coudouel, Hentschel, & Wodon 2002, p. 32). The second ingredient is choosing a poverty line. Poverty line they defined as 'cutoff points in separating the poor from non poor. They can be monetary or non monetary' and there are 'two main ways of setting poverty lines- Relative and Absolute poverty lines'(Ibid, p.33). Relative poverty line defines the position of the poor in relation to other members of the society while absolute poverty relates to those people who do not have sufficient income to afford a minimum level of nutrition and basic needs based on estimates of the cost of basic food needs (Devas, 2004).The last ingredient after defining 'wellbeing' and choosing a poverty line according to Coudouel, Hentschel & Wodon, (2002) is to choose a poverty measure to be used for the entire population. This involves a 'statistical function that translates the compared indicator of household well-being and the chosen poverty line into one aggregate number for the entire population or population sub-group' (p. 34).

The poverty line method is mostly used by the World Bank in the measurement of global poverty. However, some observers and researchers alike have accused the World Bank of underestimating poverty by using its $1 per day line and opined that a higher amount should be used, while others have asked for the line to be reduced (Ravallion, 2003). This is a further proof that there is no consensus definition and measurement of poverty. Ringen (2009) have also criticized the monetary measurement of poverty noting that the income approach to poverty measurement has failed to produce results that 'could be accepted as reliable'. He puts it thus:

"Income measures have turned out to be not persuasively sensitive to differences or changes in poverty. They have also turned out not to be robust as to the magnitude of poverty..., experiments show that minor variations in the specification and processing of income data often result in major variations in measurement results".

Finally, income measures have proved to not produce stable results that stand up to being tested against other evidence now included in the definition. The moment income data is supplemented with consumption or social indicator data, if only cautiously, measurement results tend to change strongly" (Ringen 2009, p. 3-4). One other major reason for the inadequacy of the 'income/consumption based measures' of poverty 'is that these indicators relate to the means to achieve ultimate ends rather than the ends in themselves' (Hulme,& McKay 2005, p. 4).

Other authors like Sen and Chambers have canvassed for a more qualitative and interdisciplinary approach to the measurement of poverty. These approaches goes beyond the economic growth model and looks at poverty in multidimensional ways covering all aspects of wellbeing including; capabilities, lack of freedom, and inability of the poor to participate in decision making and in the life of the community and lack of personal security(Sen 1985, 1993; Chambers 1994). Similarly, Sen's capability approach and Chambers PRA provide a great impetus to the 'bottom up approach' in measuring poverty as they focus directly on the lives that people live and what they are capable of doing.

2.3 Incidence of Poverty in Nigeria

It is true that poverty is a condition of deprivation affecting hundreds of millions of people in the world today, and this phenomenon impedes adequate human development. Unfortunately, Nigeria according to the NBS 2012 data accounts for about 112 million of the World poor. Given the vast human and natural resources that Nigeria is endowed with, and the nation's great economic potentials, poverty should not be a problem. In fact, the country should have no business with poverty. These endowments, if properly managed are capable of putting Nigeria among the richest countries of the world. Unfortunately, what occurs today is underdevelopment and massive poverty with the bulk of the country's wealth/resources residing in the hands of few elite' class who constitute an insignificant proportion of the country's population (Omotola 2008; Oshewolo 2010; Chukwuma 2013).

The above picture reaffirms Omotola 2008, argument that the endemic and high level of poverty in Nigeria is a great betrayal of her rich resources and endowments. Hence this is described in Nigeria's socio-political and economic 'lexicon' as a 'bewildering paradox' (Oshewo 2010).

Amakom (2008) records that poverty in Nigeria has many dimensions and includes 'inadequate access to government utilities and services, environmental issues, poor infrastructure, illiteracy and ignorance, poor health, insecurity, social and political exclusion' (quoted in Chukwuma, 2013, p. 2).Chukwuma, 2013 succinctly puts it thus: "The severity of poverty in Nigeria is most appreciated when viewed from its basic dimension. Rural deprivation in Nigeria constitutes one of the most basic dimensions of human misery, deprivations and poverty in the world. The poverty of rural dwellers in Nigeria is not because of lack of finance to lift them out of poverty, not because of lack of knowledge on how to go about curing the disease of poverty, but because of insincerity, corruption, cronyism and rent-seeking behaviors in governance" (Chuwuma 2013, p.3). Table 2.3.1 shows the severity of rural poverty.

Table 2.3.1: Urban/Rural Poverty incidence in Nigeria (1980 – 2004).

Poverty	Urban (%)	Rural (%)
1980	17.2	28.3
1985	37.8	51.4
1992	37.5	46.0
1996	58.2	69.3
2004	43.2	63.3

NBS, 2005

In other words, poverty was not so endemic in Nigeria prior to the 1980's. Before this period agriculture was the main stay of the Nigeria economy and people were at least able to meet their daily feeding requirements without much hassle. Also, issues of poverty were not directly part of the first, second, third and fourth development plans. Much of the focus of these plans was centered on how to make Nigeria more self reliant and less import dependent. For instance, Obadan, (2002, p. 31) noted that the poverty related issues of the 1962 to 1985 plans were centered on 'increase in per capita income; more even distribution of income; reduction in the level of unemployment; and increase in the supply of high level manpower'. As the economy became more dependent on petroleum as the main source of foreign exchange, investment in agriculture began to dwindle, thereby affecting food production and leading also to loss of agricultural labor. Thus, Enebeli- Uzor,(2009) noted that between 1970 and 2008, Nigeria's agricultural sector grew at about 1.7% per annum on average while population growth rate within the same period was 2.7%. Although, agriculture has propelled economic growth in Countries with shared developmental challenges with Nigeria in the 1960's such as Malaysia, Indonesia and Brazil, the Plethora- of challenges the sector has faced due largely to neglect has relegated the nation to become a net importer of food. Hence compounding the already bad agricultural sector bedeviled with lots of problems such as lack of proper mechanization, lack of adequate storage facilities, transportation problems, dearth of skilled manpower, the issue of availability and affordability of fertilizers, poor agric researches, over reliance on oil etc. Tables 2.3.2 and 2.3.3 showed the poverty incidence by state, and the states with the 10 highest and lowest poverty incidences in Nigeria.

Table 2.3.2: Poverty Incidence by States (1996 & 2004).

	YEARS (%)	
STATES	**1996**	**2004**
Abia	56.2	22.27
Adamawa	65.5	71.73
Akwa Ibom	66.9	34.82
Anambra	51.0	20.11
Bauchi	83.5	86.29

Bayelsa	44.3	19.98
Benue	64.2	55.33
Borno	66.9	53.63
Cross River	66.9	41.61
Delta	56.1	45.35
Ebonyi	51.0	43.33
Edo	56.1	33.09
Ekiti	71.6	42.27
Enugu	51.0	31.12
Gombe	83.5	77.01
Imo	56.2	27.39
Jigawa	71.0	95.07
Kaduna	67.7	50.24
Kano	71.0	61.29
Katsina	77.7	71.06
Kebbi	83.6	89.65
Kogi	75.5	88.55
Kwara	75.5	85.22
Lagos	53.0	63.58
Nassarawa	62.7	61.59

Niger	52.2	63.90
Ogun	69.9	31.73
Ondo	71.6	42.14
Osun	58.7	32.35
Oyo	58.7	24.08
Plateau	62.7	60.37
Rivers	44.3	29.09
Sokoto	83.9	76.81
Taraba	65.5	62.15
Yobe	66.9	83.25
Zamfara	83.9	80.93
FCT	53.0	43.32
All Nigeria	65.6	54.4

Source: NBS 2012

Table 2.3.3 Poverty Incidence in Nigeria by 10 Different States with Highest & Lowest Poverty Rate.

	10 states with highest poverty incidence (%)	Poverty incidence (%)	10 states with lowest poverty incidence (%)	Poverty incidence (%)
1.	Jigawa	95.0	Bayelsa	20.0
2.	Kebbi	89.7	Anambra	20.1
3.	Kogi	88.6	Abia	22.3
4.	Bauchi	86.3	Oyo	24.1
5.	Kwara	85.2	Imo	27.4

6.	Yobe	83.3	Rivers	29.1
7.	Zamfara	80.9	Enugu	31.1
8.	Gombe	77.0	Ogun	31.7
9.	Sokoto	76.8	Osun	32.4
10.	Adamawa	71.7	Edo	33.1

Source: NBS, 2005.

The problems of poverty started to increase from the middle of 1980's when the SAP a reform program adopted by the General Ibrahim Babangida in 1986 to remedy the already ailing economy failed to stabilize the economy. The SAP led to further deteriorating economic and social conditions for the vulnerable group (the poor) of the Nigerian people (Uniamikogbo, 1997; Obadan 2002).

Since then, the country has continued to witness high level of both income and human poverty making successive governments as we shall see later to promulgate different anti-poverty policies aimed towards reducing poverty in Nigeria. Today, Nigeria's social and economic indicators are among the worst in the World (see table 2.3.4) and the country is lagging behind in all indices of development. In terms of educational development, provision of basic needs of life like roads, housing, water, health care and transportation Nigeria ranks among the most back-ward in the World. For instance, the World Health Organization (WHO) and United Nations Children's Fund (UNICEF) joint monitoring program in its 2012 progress report on drinking water and sanitation ranked Nigeria as third on the list of countries with the highest number of population without improved drinking water. The report stated that 66 million Nigerians do not have access to clean drinking water, while 34 million people, about 20% of the population practice open defecation (Okpi, 2012). Similarly, the National Bureau of Statistics, reports that the percentage of Nigerians living in absolute poverty increased from 54.4% in 2004 to 60.9% in 2010 (Subair, 2012).

Similarly, Daouda Toure, the representative of the United Nations Development Program (UNDP) in Nigeria alluded to the growing level of poverty and unemployment in Nigeria at the 53rd annual conference of the Nigeria Economic Society. He raised serious concerns about the increasing level of poverty and unemployment in the country and lamented why the almost one decade of consistent economic growth has not produced commensurate employment generation and poverty reduction for her citizens (The Nation, 2012).

Also, a recent Global competitiveness report released by the World Economic Forum ranked Nigeria's Economy as the 99th in the world among 133 Countries assessed by the forum. The forum also ranked Nigeria in terms of security, corruption, wasteful expenditure, health and primary education where it is placed in the 117th, 122nd, 127th, and 132nd positions respectively among 133 nations. The World Bank and the International Finance Corporation also ranked Nigeria 125th among 183 economics in the world in terms of the general regulatory case of doing business (Tell 2009). Udeh (2000) also noted that estimates of Nigeria's earning from oil export receipts between 1981 and 1999 are put at US$228 billion. Yet the number of Nigerians living in abject poverty, that is, on less than $1 a day doubled between 1970 and 2000.It rose from 36% in 1970 to 70% in 2000.Nigeria's per capita income of US$370 in 2000 is much less than its level of US$780, in the 1980s (Iyoha 2005).

Table 2.3.4: Human Development Index for Some Selected Countries

Country	Life expectancy at birth		Infant mortality rate		Adult literacy rate		Population with access to safe water	
	1960	1994	1960	1994	1970	1994	1990	2002
Ghana	45.0	56.6	189	82	31	63	54	70
Indonesia	41.2	63.5	139	53	83	94	71	78
Kenya	44.7	53.6	124	70	33	62	45	62
Morocco	46.7	63.3	163	58	22	42	75	80
Nigeria	39.5	51.0	189	82	25	56	49	60
South Africa	49.0	63.7	89	51	-	-	83	87

Source: Human Development Report (1997 and 2005)

2.4 Poverty Reduction Strategies in Nigeria

This section reviews some of the past strategies and programs initiated by the federal government of Nigeria towards poverty alleviation. Much of these policies and programs were more focused on economic growth, basic needs and rural development. Also worthy of note here is that much of the poverty alleviation strategies initiated before 1994 when the Poverty Alleviation Program Development Committee (PAPDC) was inaugurated by the federal government 'were essentially ad-hoc' because much of the programs were not integrated and consolidated within the country's general 'development objectives' (Obadan 2002). Before the inception of SAP in Nigeria, some policy measures were introduced which was geared mainly towards human resources development and poverty reduction. The government then realized the importance of human capital development in economic development and poverty reduction. Hence the implementation of the national policy on education was vigorously pursued (Uniamikogbo, 1997).

Similarly, during and after the SAP era a lot of policies and programs were formulated and implemented to impact directly on the lives of the poor. In 1986, the Directorate of Food, Roads and Rural Infrastructures (DFRRI) was established. The aim of DFRRI was to address the problems of rural poverty by providing requisite infrastructures like roads, electricity, schools, pipe borne water etc. In 1987 the National Directorate of Employment (NDE) was lunched to try to provide employment opportunities for the youths and make them more self-reliant. The government, in realizing the role of finance to poverty reduction created the Peoples Bank of Nigeria in 1989 and the Community Banking in 1990. The later was meant to focus specifically on the rural areas. In all, the banks were meant to provide loans to low income individuals who participate actively in the informal sector. Other programs during this era include; the Family Support Program (FSP); The Better Life Program (BLP) and the Family Economic Advancement Program (FEAP). The FSP and BSP were established to provide health care services, child welfare; youth empowerment and enhance the quality of lives of women in the rural areas, while the FEAP objectives was to provide credit facilities to cooperative societies in both rural and urban areas to establish cottage industries (Uniamikogbo, 1997; Obadan, 2002 Ogwumike, 2002).

Recent governments since 1999 when Nigeria returned to civil rule have also made effort to reduce poverty by formulating different policies and programs. When Olusegun Obasanjo assumed office as President in 1999, he saw the issue of poverty as a grave and serious problem confronting the government and people of Nigeria. This recognition led the government to take series of measures to fight the scourge. Some of such measures were the establishment of the Universal Basic Education (UBE) and National Poverty Eradication Program (NAPEP) and the streamlining and rationalization of all previous anti poverty programs under different agencies of government under the NAPEP with a view to avoidable duplication of functions, wastage and improved institutional performance. The UBE program was aimed at providing free and compulsory primary and junior secondary education to the Nigeria Child. This was occasioned by the fact that education is a veritable tool in poverty reduction. Similarly, the NAPEP Program was focused on key strategic areas which includes; employment, training and skill acquisition, primary health care delivery, special education; rural development and micro-credit delivery (FRN, 2001).

Finally, one troubling point to note is that despite the plethora of anti poverty programs/policies established/created in Nigeria over the years, the problem of poverty remains unabated. That is poverty is still increasing in Nigeria instead of reducing. This is why I have argued that poverty statistics of Sub Saharan Africa is growing because of the failure of the government to reduce the plague in Nigeria. Other big giants like China and Brazil have succeeded in reducing poverty in their different climes to the barest minimum through ensuring purposeful implementation of anti poor policies and ensuring proper distribution of societal resources and ensuring inclusive growth.

For this reason, for any anti poverty program to work successfully in Nigeria, the governments among other things must shone corruption, nepotism and political bickering and truly focus on purposeful and altruistic governance by ensuring that people at the epicenter of development actually feel the impact of their policies. Hence, a study of this type which focuses on impact of microfinance could be a veritable tool for poverty reduction if properly implemented.

CHAPTER THREE

Conceptual Issues in Microfinance

> *Microfinance has proven to be an effective and powerful tool for poverty reduction. Like many other development tools, however, it has insufficiently penetrated the poorer strata of society. The poorest form the vast majority of those without access to primary health care and basic education; similarly, they are the majority of those without access to microfinance.*
>
> -Morduch & Haley (2002).

This chapter focuses on the discussion of the Microfinance framework and its impact on poverty reduction. Specific attention will be on the overview, definition and meaning, growth of microfinance in Nigeria, the justification for the establishment of MFB's in Nigeria and finally a review of some empirical literatures on microfinance and theoretical framework for the study.

3.1 General Overview of Microfinance/Microcredit Scheme

Since the establishment of the Gramaen Bank by Mohamed Yunus in 1976 microfinance have continued to receive great international attention especially amongst different national governments, international NGO's, international financial organizations like the World Bank and IMF and also the United Nations.

It is believed that Microfinance has existed (although in different form) for centuries, long before the establishments and growth of modern microfinance banks (Midgley, 2008; Ehigiamusoe 2011). The poor for centuries have always had access to loans especially from local money lenders (Midgley, 2008). According to Siebel 2004 (quoted in Ehigiamusoe 2011), all major developed countries of today have their own history of microfinance. He explained that both formal and informal institutions have been in existence to deliver credits to low income people. Siebel traced the existence of community based financial transactions in West Africa to the 16th century, and explained that these thrifts and credits groups were organized around 'kinship and age grade systems before the introduction of the co-operative thrifts and credit societies to Africa later in the early 20th century.

Furthermore, the declaration by the United Nations pronouncing 2005 the year of microcredit and the 2006 Noble Peace Prize award to Dr. Mohamed Yunus, the founder of Gramaen Bank gave further impetus to the growth of microfinance globally (Midgley, 2008). For instance, by 2009 microfinance had spread to many countries across five continents of the world leading to the duplication of the Gramaen bank model in many countries like Bolivia, Chile; China, Ethiopia, Nigeria, Honduras, India, Malaysia, Mali, the Philippines, Sri Lanka, Tanzania, Thailand, the United States and Vietnam (Tseng 2011, p. 149). Similarly, this growth was also reinforced by the believe of World Leaders that microfinance was a major tool/instrument that will help in the realization of the target of the millennium development goal of halving poverty by 2015. It was believed that microfinance will help provide credits to poor households majorly excluded from accessing loans from formal financial institutions due to a number of factors including; high interest rate, collateral requirements, complicated application procedures and cumbersome bureaucratic processes (Tseng 2011).

Since 2005/2006 microfinance started to witness a high growth in terms of numbers of MFI's and the clients they serve. According to the State of Microcredit Summit Campaign Report 2012 (see table 3.1.1) as at 2010 there were 3,652 MFI's in the World serving a total of 205,314,502 clients as against 190,135,080 clients in 2009. These MFI's also served a total of 137,547,441 poorest clients in 2010 out of which 113,138,652 were women representing about 82.25%. A breakdown of the report shows that 82.4% of the clients are from the Asia/Pacific region while 6.7% are from Latin America/Caribbean; Sub-Saharan Africa accounts for 6.2%, 2.1 are from Middle East/North Africa while the remaining 2.6% are from the Industrialized World.

Table 3.1.1: Global Microfinance Statistics (2009-2010)

Region	Number of Programs Reporting	Number Of Total in 2009	Number Of Total in 2010	Number of Poorest Clients in 2009	Number of Poorest Clients in 2010	Number of Poorest Women Clients in 2009	Number of Poorest Women Clients in 2010
Sub-Saharan Africa	1,009	10,776,726	12,692,579	6,360,861	7,248,732	3,935,808	4,783,256
Asia and Pacific	1,746	156,403,658	169,125,878	117,178,142	125,530,437	97,385,541	104,752,430
Latin America & Caribbean	647	12,257,181	13,847,987	2,834,742	2,919,646	1,935,685	2,363,100
Middle East & North Africa	91	4,552,387	4,290,735	1,492,322	1,680,181	1,217,113	1,165,358
Developing World Totals	3,493	183,989,952	199,957,179	127,866,067	137,378,996	104,474,146	113,064,144
North America & Western Europe	86	148,628	155,254	109,318	41,809	56,651	12,214
Eastern Europe & Central Asia	73	5,996,500	5,202,069	233,810	126,636	163,318	62,294
IndustrializedWorld	159	6,145,128	5,357,323	343,128	168,445	219,969	74,508
Global Total	3,652	190,135,080	205,314,502	128,209,195	137,547,441	104,694,115	113,138,652

Source: State of the Microcredit Summit Campaign Report 2012

3.2 Definition and Meaning of Microfinance

The term, microfinance have been defined in different ways by different authors. Midgley (2008, p.468) defines microfinance as the provision of small credit to poor people usually with 'little or no collateral and at a comparatively low interest rate'. Ikechukwu (2012, p.107) conceives microfinance as a poverty reduction strategy which is aimed at providing loans 'and other financial services to economically active and low income households and their businesses'.

According to Mohammed Yunus (2003), Microfinance involves the process of giving access to financing to as many poor people as possible, allowing them to utilize their capacities in favor of lasting development (quoted in Dobra 2011, p.135). For Ehigiamusoe (2011), the practice of microfinance does not only mean disbursement and collection of loan repayment and savings, it equally refers to a set of less rigid organization structures and procedures by which necessary financial services are provided to low-income people and owners of small enterprises on a sustainable basis. It can be deduce from the above definitions that microfinance is basically about providing loans and credit to the poor who are usually excluded from the normal banking system in the society. For our purpose; Microfinance is defined as the process whereby small loans and credits including other financial products are specially provided to the poor people in the society to enable them engage in micro business/enterprises and other profitable ventures.

The aim of microfinance is the same across the world-to instigate entrepreneurial interest in the poor thus making them to generate income for themselves and be able to live a life of 'meaningful wellbeing'. According to Ehigiamusoe (2011), microfinance practices have some common features across the world. He identified some common elements of microfinance as below;

- Collateral Substitution; that is all MFB does tend to disregard tangible collateral security.
- Small Units of Services; that is clients of MFB's owns small enterprises.
- High cost of Transactions; here he explained that MFB's operations involve high cost of transactions and little returns on investment.
- Priorities focus on Women; that is women constitute the majority of clients of MFB's usually up to 80% of clients base in different parts of the world.
- Group Methodology; This involves people coming together to form a group(union) and accessing credit as a member of the group, but take individual responsibility for the utilization and repayment of the loans collected.
- Clientele; that is clients of MFB's are usually the poor or low-income people and their micro-enterprises
- Access to Repeat Loans; that is borrowers are allowed to take loans over a number of cycles with each new cycle having a higher amount than the previous. However, only credit worthy clients with demonstrated capacity and good character have access to larger loans (Ehigiamusoe 2011, p 5-13).

3.3 Growth of Microfinance in Nigeria

> *In 2005, the share of micro credit as a percentage of total credit was 0.9%, while it contributed a meager 0.2 Percent of the GDP*
>
> -Bamisile (2006).

As already stated, before the emergence of modern microfinance institutions in Nigeria, there already existed different kinds of traditional institutional set ups that offer microfinance services in Africa. This is particularly true of Nigeria where indigenous traditional savings and credits groups existed- like Adashi in the North and Isusu, Osusu, and Esusu in the South of the country

(Ehigiamusoe, 2011). Most of these savings and credits groups still exist in some parts of the country although no longer widespread. The emergence of modern microfinance started in the 1980's with the establishment of the People's bank, community bank, Family support program, family economic advancement program and others by the government. This was also supported by increased activities of donor agencies, NGO's, credit unions, moneylenders, etc. These groups delivered credits to relatively poor members of their immediate environment (LAPO, 2009, CBN, 2011).

In 2005, the Central Bank of Nigeria launched the Microfinance Policy, Supervisory and Regulatory Framework. This policy framework was aimed at increasing the access of microenterprises and micro-entrepreneurs to credits and financial services to boost their businesses and contribute to national economic growth (CBN, 2005). The formulation of this law has led to the growth of MFB'S/MFI's in Nigeria with over 800 registered MFB's scattered across the country. This law according to CBN provides for the establishment of three different categories of MFB's in Nigeria;

- Category 1: Unit Microfinance Bank, is licensed to operate in one designated location without having any branch and must have a minimum initial capital of N20 million (twenty million Naira) that is about $125,000 deposited with the CBN.
- Category 2: the State Microfinance Bank is registered to operate within one state or the Federal Capital Territory (FCT). MFB's in this category are expected to have a minimum paid up capital of N100 million (one hundred million Naira) about $625,000.
- Category 3: National Microfinance Bank. Is licensed and authorized to operate in all states of the country including the FCT, but must have a minimum capital of N2 billion (two billion Naira) which is about $125,000,000.

The microfinance policy was aimed at achieving the following objectives: Helping in ensuring the provision of different, affordable and dependable financial services to the economically active poor who otherwise could not access loans to develop their entrepreneurial activities. Also to help create employment opportunities and increase the productivity of the active poor in the country, consequently enhancing their living standards and capabilities. The policy also aimed at promoting synergy and mainstreaming of the informal microfinance sub-sector into the formal financial system, thereby ensuring active participation of the poor in socio-economic development and resource allocation. Lastly, is the mobilization of savings for intermediation, contribution to rural transformation and equally promotion of linkage programs between MFI's, Deposit Money Banks, Development Financial Institutions and Specialized Funding Institutions (CBN, 2011).

3.4 Justification for the Establishment of Microfinance Banks in Nigeria

According to the CBN, the justifications for the establishment of the Microfinance Policy was due largely to the abysmal failure of the erstwhile community banks and microfinance NGO's in providing adequate finance or credit to the poor. Their failure was as a result of some factors which includes; Poor performance and incompetent management, poor corporate governance, weak internal controls and lack of deposit insurance schemes. Also they had a poor capital base which was not adequate enough to cover for loses and provide a cover for the risk of lending to micro-enterprises. Similarly, the un-served financial market was so huge, hence necessitating a broader framework that would ensure adequate provision of financial services and credits to millions of Nigerians without access to banking services. According to a 2008 finance survey in Nigeria, 79 percent of the total population and 86 percent of the rural population is unbanked. Also, in 2005, the aggregate microcredit facilities in Nigeria accounted for a meager 0.2 percent of GDP and less than one percent of total credit to the economy (CBN 2005; 2011).Hence, the main target group of the policy were the very poor and illiterates who resides in the rural areas who were hitherto not able to have any banking relationship because of finance illiteracy, remoteness from bank locations and complete ignorance of what banking entails (CBN 2005, 2011, Ehigiamusoe 2011).

Lastly, there was the need to attract private investments into the sector in order to reduce the 'Urban bias in banking services' and have more MFB's established in the rural areas so as to promote increased economic empowerment of the poor by increasing their saving opportunities and ultimately having a better life.

3.5 Empirical Literatures on Microfinance

There have been diverse opinions by scholars and researchers alike about the usefulness, effectiveness and impact of microfinance on poverty reduction. Several studies already conduct-

ed on this subject matter concluded with positive results while others had mixed results. Therefore, this section presents a review of some empirical studies on microfinance:
In a survey of ten major microfinance institutions titled *Microfinance Institutions in Nigeria: Policy Practice and Potentials* Anyanwu (2004), discovered that the MFI's have grown tremendously in the past ten years in Nigeria due to expanding informal sector activities and the reluctance of normal banks to fund the emerging micro-enterprises. The study discovered a number of challenges militating against the operations of MFI 's as follows: Inability of the MFI's to reach a large number of the poor, Poor funding of the real sector, especially agriculture and manufacturing production. These sectors he noted received only 14.1% and 3.5% respectively, while the commerce sector got the bulk of 78.4% of the total MFI's funding. It was also discovered that the level of financial self sufficiency of the MFI's were low as they relied heavily more on grants rather than on savings as a source of funding.

Lafourcade, Et al (2005) in a study of the overview of the outreach and financial performance of microfinance institutions in Africa reported that MFI's in Africa have witnessed tremendous expansion in recent years and that many unregulated microfinance institutions are reaching poorer clients, but the problem is that they have limited coverage. Compared to other regions of the world, the study found out that MFI's in Africa rely greatly on clients savings as a source of fund for lending to clients. In terms of profit it was revealed that Africa MFI's recorded lower levels of profitability compared to other regions of the world. Lafourcade, Et al revealed that despite the growth of MFI's in Africa they are still bedeviled with lots of challenges like high operating and financial expenses, low efficiency in terms of cost per borrower and poor technological application. Hence they opined that technological innovation, products refinement and other efforts are needed to reduce cost, increase outreach and boost overall profitability.

Similarly, the findings of a study by Charles and Hamid (2005) of the influence of loan disbursement by microfinance and non microfinance institutions on poverty alleviation in Nigeria revealed a difference between users and non users of microcredit. Their results also showed that there was great impact of microfinance institutions credits on poverty alleviating and that there was increased income and changing economic status of those who patronized MFI's. They concluded by noting that microfinance can be more viable if the outreach of the program is well enhanced beyond its present reach.

Furthermore, a study of the Effectiveness of Microfinance Banks in Alleviating Poverty in Kwara State of Nigeria by Yahaya, Osemene & Abdulraheem (2011) showed that microfinance helps in reducing poverty by providing financial services to the poor, generating employment and assisting small businesses to grow. The study however recommended that regulatory authorities should look at the interest rate charged on loans by the MFB's which is very high so as to make credit more affordable to the active poor. They also recommended that the government should ensure the provision of basic infrastructures like roads, water and electricity as this would greatly impact on the output of micro-entrepreneurs.

Furthermore, Table 3.5.1 shows a summary of some other empirical works on microfinance in Asia and Latin adopted from Montgomery and Weiss (2005). Most of the findings revealed a positive improvement in the income and welfare of borrowers compared with the controlled group. For instance Pitt and Khandlers (1998) study of three MFI's in Bangladesh revealed 'Positive impact of program participation on total weekly expenditure per capita', increased women's labor supply and 'strong effect of female participation in Grameen Bank on schooling of girls'. However, there was no direct proof of any impact on the lives of the extreme poor and also that extremely poor do not have more access to finance compared to the relatively richer clients. Also, Mosley (2001) study of selected MFB's in Bolivia discovered that Growth of incomes and assets of borrowers always exceeds that of control group. Increase in borrowers' income larger for better-off borrowers. No evidence of impact on 'extreme poverty.

Table 3.5.1: Summary of some of Empirical Work in Asia and Latin America

Study	Coverage	Methodology	Results
Hulme and Mosley (1996)	Indonesia (BKK, KURK, BRI), Bangladesh (Grameen, BRAC, TRDEP), Sri lanka (PTCCS)	Borrowers and controls samples, before and after.	Growth of incomes of borrowers always exceeds that of control group. Increase in borrowers' income larger for better-off borrowers.
Khandler (1998)	Bangladesh (Grameen, BRAC)	Double difference comparison between eligible and ineligible households and	5% of participant households removed from poverty annually. Additional

		between programme and non-programme villages.	consumption of 18 taka for every 100 taka of loan taken out by women.
Pitt and Khandlers (1998)	Bangladesh (BRAC, BRDB, Grameen Bank)	Double difference estimation between eligible and non-eligible households and programmes with and without microfinance programmes. Estimations are conducted separately for male and female borrowing.	Positive impact of programme participation on total weekly expenditure per capita, women's labour supply. Strong effect of female participation in Grameen Bank on schooling of girls. Credit programmes can change village attitudes and other village characteristics.
Hulme and Mosley (1996)	Bolivia, BancoSol	Borrowing and control samples, before and after. Retrospective assessment of incomes.	Growth of incomes of borrowers always exceeds that of control group. Absolute increase in borrowers' income larger for better-off borrowers.
Mosley (2001)	Bolivia, BancoSo, ProMujer, PRODEM and SARTAWA	Borrowers and control samples, before and after. Times series data for BancoSol only; for other retrospective assessment of incomes.	Growth of incomes and assets of borrowers always exceeds that of control group. Increase in borrowers income larger for better-off borrowers. No evidence of impact on 'extreme poverty.'

Source: Adapted from Montgomery and Weiss (2005)

3.6 Theoretical Framework

The theoretical framework used in this study is Capability Approach.

Capability Approach

The Capability Approach has been pioneered by Amartya Sen-a renowned economist, Philosopher and a Nobel Laureate. It has also been recently developed by Martha Nussbaum and other notable Scholars (Robeyns, 2005). This approach explains poverty not in monetary sense (income and consumption) but as a result of deprivation or lack of basic capability to live a valuable life. In other words, living a life of adequate wellbeing requires meeting some basic capabilities and functioning (see Sen, 1983, 1984, 1985; 1988, 1993, 1999).

Sen (1988) posits that so long as development is concerned with the achievement of a better life its focus of analysis should include the kind of life people 'succeed in living'. He puts it thus; *The nature of the life that people succeed in living in each period is also a matter of importance. People value their ability to do certain things and to achieve certain types of beings (such as being well nourished, being free from avoidable morbidity; being able to move about as desired an so on). These doings and beings may me be generically called functioning of a person...,the wellbeing of a person can be seen as an evaluation of the functioning achieved by that person* (Sen 1988, p. 15). Sen also noted that the achievement of functioning does not depend only on the commodities a person have, but the availability of some certain public goods needed to achieve a certain functioning. For instance, achieving good health, literacy and adequate nourishment depends on the corresponding provision of the necessary public goods like good health and medical facilities, schools (Sen 1988, p. 16). Hence, the capability approach analyses policies based on their impact on the capabilities of the people and also identify social constraints that inhibit living a life of adequate wellbeing (Robeyns, 2005).

The capability approach is very useful in explaining the nature of poverty in Nigeria and why the menace is increasing. For instance it would be a wild dream to think that a child that was deprived the necessary basic capability of having basic education and be literate to have the basic skills necessary to live a life of adequate wellbeing. Consequently, this study examines poverty within this framework by focusing on the failure of the government to provide for the citizens especially the poor the needed capabilities and functioning to live a life of meaningful wellbeing.

Unemployment, corruption, non-diversification of the economy, poor social amenities and weak/decrepit infrastructural and poor leadership has contributed to exacerbate the problem of poverty in Nigeria. These combined problems have greatly deprive the people the needed wherewithal and capability to live a meaningful life of 'adequate wellbeing'. I therefore argue that for the microfinance to adequately meet its aim of adequate poverty reduction on a large scale in Nigeria the above problems must be tackled.

Furthermore, the capability approach is very much synonymous with the rights based theory that sees poverty as a violation of the human rights of the poor. Martha Nussbaum, 2003 also shares this view. According to her, the capability approach is closely related to the Universal human rights. These rights she added are those that have to do with 'opportunities and capabilities' that enable an individual to make choices about life's plan, and that the fundamental human rights can only be meaningful when people have the desired capability to function. She puts it thus:

> *Regarding fundamental rights, I would argue that the best way of thinking about what it is to secure them to people is to think in terms of capabilities. The right to political participation, the right to religious free exercise, the right of free speech – these and others are all best thought of as secured to people only when the relevant capabilities to function are present. In other words, to secure a right to citizens in these areas is to put them in a position of capability to function in that area. To the extent that rights are used in defining social justice, we should not grant that the society is just unless the capabilities have been effectively achieved* (Nussbaum 2003, p.37).

CHAPTER FOUR

Research Methodology

4.1 Research Design

Every empirical work has its own specific research design that acts as an 'action plan' for the research. According to Yin, (1984) a research design is the logical sequence that "connects the empirical data to a study's initial research questions and ultimately to its conclusions..., It is a blueprint of research dealing with at least four problems: what questions to study, what data are relevant, what data to collect, and how to analyze the results" (pp.28-29).
This study adopted survey research in sourcing for data and makes use of both qualitative and quantitative methods of data collection. Survey research is the process of collecting data from a large sample of people determined from a population of interest that a researcher has chosen for a particular study and the researcher uses the information from the sample 'to make some inference about the wider population' (Kelley Et al 2003, p.261). The choice of a survey research for this study is predicated on the fact that it allows for the collection of data from relatively large population and also to allow the use of diverse methods of data collection.

Also, given the intricate and controversial nature of the question of microfinance and poverty, it is appropriate to use diverse methods because the weakness of one method can be 'compensated by the counter-balancing strengths of another' and this gives room for getting a variety of data which 'can lead to an enriched explanation of the research problem'(Jick, 1979).

4.2 The Area of Study

Benin Metropolis is the area of study for this research. The metropolis is made up of three local government areas: Oredo, Ikpoba-Okha and Egor with a combined population (according to the 2006 Census figures) of 1,086,882 people. That is 374,515; 372,080 and 340,287 for the three local government areas respectively. The inhabitants of the area are the Benin ethnic groups and settlers from other parts of the country. Benin metropolis is one of most cosmopolitan cities in Nigeria with some tertiary educational institutions (like the University of Benin, Benson Idahosa University and College of Education, Ekiadolor), Agro allied industries, breweries and host of other state and federal government institutions. Benin metropolis is home to the Benin Kingdom:

one of the most famous empires in West Africa during the pre-colonial era. The area known for its rich cultural heritage is popularly referred to as the land of arts and culture and is very rich in cultural artifacts such as wood carving, blacksmithing, ivory works, bronze casting among others (Ugiagbe, 2012).

4.3 Population of Study

The population of study is all the people that have previously accessed loan/microcredit from microfinance banks in Benin metropolis. This is without any gender bias.

4.4 Sample

The respondents in this study were selected using the cluster sampling. Benin metropolis was divided into its constituent parts: Oredo, Ikpoba-Okha and Egor. From the lists of microfinance banks in the area, two each were selected from Oredo and Ikpoba-Okha, while one was picked from Egor. This selection was done based on population and concentration of microfinance banks in the respective local government areas. Being that Oredo and Ikpoba-Okha have more population and microfinance banks two each were selected from there why one was picked from Egor. Thereafter, 50 clients were randomly selected from each of the MFB's making it 250 clients/respondents that the questionnaire/interview guide was administered to (see table 4.4.1 for breakdown of sample frame).

Table 4.4.1: Breakdown of Sample Frame

Name of LGA'S	NUMBER OF MFB'S SELECTED	NUMBER OF CLIENTS SELECTED
Oredo	2	2x50= 100
Ikpoba- Okha	2	2x50=100
Egor	1	1x50=50
Total	5	250

Among the 250 samples selected for the questionnaire, 80 percent which is 200 was valid. Most of the respondents were not willing to fill the questions and others were not correctly filled, hence were discarded.

4.5 Sample Size

The sample size for this study was two hundred and sixty five (265) people (Male and female) who have accessed micro-credits and heads/managers of selected microfinance banks in the study area. Fifty (50) invalid questionnaires were discarded hence 200 was retained for analysis. Also five (5) other people who are heads of microfinance banks selected each from the respective MFB's studied were subjected to structured in-depth interviews, and another 10 beneficiaries of micro-credits who are leaders of selected unions were subjected to focus group interviews/discussion. Therefore, the total valid sample size for the study was two hundred and fourteen (215) respondents.

4.6 Methods of Data Collection

This study collected data from both primary and secondary sources. The primary means of data includes questionnaire, structured interview, focus group interviews/discussions and participant observation.

Questionnaire

Questionnaire was one of the sources used in collecting data for this study. An already existing instrument/questionnaire was used to collect data. This is sequel to the fact raised by Punch (2005) that using a good already existing questionnaire helps to save time and resources and that the more a particular questionnaire/instrument is used, 'the more we learn about its properties'. Also, using an existing questionnaire/instrument makes it possible for research results from different studies to be 'more easily compared, integrated and synthesized' (Punch 2005, p.93).
The questionnaires were administered with support by two research assistants who were trained for two days about the contents of the questionnaire, how to interact with respondents and also how to collect and record their responses. During the process of administering the questionnaires it was discovered that many of the respondents were not literate. Hence, those that were literate enough were given the questionnaires to complete on their own, why the non literate ones were assisted to complete it by reading and explaining the questions succinctly to them. The respond-

ents were accessed at the offices of selected microfinance banks (where they come daily for different transactions) after due approval from the management of the banks. In other words, Strict confidentiality was adhered to in administering the questionnaires and there was no interference by staff of the MFB's.

Structured Interview

Structured interview was carried out on five (5) selected heads/directors of microfinance banks. It was conducted using a pre-structured interview guide. The essence of this method was to have different views from those of the clients and also to have an understanding of the management processes of these organizations, including the challenges and regulatory framework guiding the operations of the MFB's. Importantly also, it's 'stimulus- response nature' enhances rational instead of 'emotional responses' (Fontana & Frey, 1994 quoted in Punch 2005, p.170) and allowed for comparism of the data gotten from other sources.

Focus Group Discussion

FGD involves the interviewing of different respondents at the same time rather than one person. According to Punch (2005), FGD interviews helps to bring out some important information which might otherwise not exposed by the respondent and the group situation also stimulate the respondents in making their views more succinct. Consequent upon the above, conducting FGD in this study was useful in crosschecking other information or data already collected thereby making the results more reliable. Ten (10) respondents who are beneficiaries of micro-credits and heads of microfinance unions in the five MFB's of study were selected for the FGD.

Participant Observation

The aim of participant observation was to physically observe the proceedings of the MFB's union meeting with a view to getting other useful information not gotten from other sources. I participated in one union meeting of over 40 members.

Secondary Data

In addition to the primary data sourced for this work, a lot of other secondary data were also used in this study, these includes: government policies and program documents, annual reports and other publications of MFB's, journal articles and books that have direct relevance to the study.

4.7 Data Analysis

The data collected in this study was analyzed using descriptive statistics and simple percentage. Tabulations and charts were also used. The raw data was processed using SPSS

CHAPTER FIVE

Data Analysis, Interpretation and Discussions of Results

This chapter analyzes the data gathered during the field work of this study carried out through administration of questionnaires, In-depth oral interviews, Focus Group Discussions and Participant Observation. The questions were entirely examined while tables were used for the analysis followed by the interpretation.

To ensure a clear and succinct presentation, the data result of this study was presented in the following order of four different questions:

Question one: The socio-economic and demographic characteristics of microfinance scheme beneficiaries.

Question two: The impact of microfinance on the living standard and wellbeing of the beneficiaries

Question three: The policies, regulatory and supervisory frameworks which guide microfinance banks in Nigeria

Question four: The general constraints hampering the successful implementation of the micro-finance scheme.

5.1 Question one: Socio-Economic and Demographic Characteristics of Microfinance Scheme Beneficiaries

The tables below show the socio-economic and demographic characteristics of MFB beneficiaries in the study area.

Table 5.1.1: Age of Respondents

Age	Frequency	Percent
Below 20 years	10	5.0
21-40 years	110	55.0
41-60 years	55	27.5
Above 60 years	25	12.5
Total	**200**	**100.0**

Source: Field Work, 2012

From The above table, out of 200 respondents only 10 (5.0%) respondents are below 20 years, while 21-40 years old respondents are 110 (55.0%), then 41-60 years old are 55 (27.5%) and above 60 years old are 25 (12.5%).

Table 5.1.2: Sex of Respondents

Sex	Frequency	Percent
Male	23	11.5
Females	177	88.5
Total	**200**	**100.0**

Source: Field Work, 2012

Table 5.1.2 shows that 23(11.5) respondents were Men, while females were 177(88.5).This result corroborate the fact that Microcredit beneficiaries are predominantly Women.

Table 5.1.3: Marital Status of Respondents

Marital Status	Frequency	Percent
Single	42	21.0
Married	124	62.0
Separated	18	9.0
Widowed	16	8.0
Total	**200**	**100.0**

Source: Field Work, 2012

Table 5.1.3 above, shows that 42 respondents (21.0%) are singles while married respondents are 124 (62.0%) then 18 (9.0%) respondents said they are separated and 16 (8.0%) said they are widow. This means that majority of the clients/respondents are those who belong to the married class.

Table 5.1.4: Education Background of Respondents

Education Background	Frequency	Percent
None	40	20.0
Primary School Leaving Certificate	50	25.0
Junior Secondary	10	5.0
Senior Secondary/NECO/GCE	40	20.0
National Diploma/NCE	31	15.5
HND/First Degree	20	10.0
Maser/Ph.D.	9	4.5
Total	**200**	**100.0**

Source: Field Work, 2012

From the above table, 40 (20.0%) said none (that is no education background), while 50(25.0%) had primary education then 10 (5.0%) had junior secondary school education, 40 (20.0%) had senior secondary education, 31 (15.5%) had only National Diploma/NCE, 20 (10.0%) had HND/First Degree and 9(4.5%) had Master/Ph.D. This indicates that most of the clients/respondents of the MFB's have average Primary Education and Secondary Education.

Table 5.1.5: Religion of Respondents

Religion	Frequency	Percent
Christianity	145	72.5
Islam	23	11.5
Others	32	16.0
Total	**200**	**100.0**

Source: Field Work, 2012

Table 5.1.5 above shows that 145 respondents (72.5%) are Christians while Muslims respondents are 23 (11.5%) and respondents who said others are 32 (16.0%). This means that majority of the microcredit beneficiaries (respondents) are from the Christian faith. This supports the fact that majority of the people living in Benin Metropolis are predominantly Christians.

Table 5.1.6: Occupation of Respondents

Occupation	Frequency	Percent
Trading/Business	150	75.0
Civil Service Work	20	10.0
Teaching	3	1.5
Driver	2	1.0
Security	2	1.0
Bike Rider	2	1.0
Marketing	5	2.5
Students	8	4.0
Furniture	6	3.0
None	2	1.0
Total	**200**	**100.0**

Source: Field Work, 2012

From the above table, 150 (75.0%) respondents are Traders/Business, while 20 (10.0%) respondents are civil servants then 3 (1.5%) respondents are teachers, 2 (1.5%) are drivers, security, Bike riders and those who said none, 5 (2.5%) are marketers, 8 (4.0%) are students and 6 (3.0%) are furniture makers. This evidence replicates the fact that majority of microcredit beneficiaries use their loans for trading and business.

Table 5.1.7: How many times have you borrowed from Micro-Finance Institution(s)

Variable	Frequency	Percent
Once	62	31.0
Twice	32	16.0
More than twice	106	53.0
Total	**200**	**100.0**

Source: Field Work, 2012

From the above table, 62 (31.0%) respondents claim they have borrowed once while 32 (16.0%) respondents claim they have borrowed twice and 106 (53%) respondents claim they have borrowed more than twice.

Table 5.1.8: How many of your children are still in school

Variable	Frequency	Percent
None	81	40.5
1-3	81	40.5
Above 4	38	19.0
Total	**200**	**100.0**

Source: Field Work, 2012

From the above table, 81 (40.5%) respondents said none of their children are in school while 81 (40.5%) respondents said 1-3 of their children are still in school and 38 (19.0%) respondents said above 4 of their children are still in school.

5.2 Question two: The Impact of Microfinance on the Living Standard and Wellbeing of the Beneficiaries

The data generated to measure the assessments of the impacts of micro credits on beneficiaries are presented below:

Table 5.2.1: I feed better than I used to do

Variable	Frequency	Percent
Strongly Agree (SA)	48	24.0
Agree (A)	114	57.0
Strongly Disagree (SD)	13	6.5
Disagree (D)	20	10.0
None	5	2.5
Total	**200**	**100.0**

Source: Field Work, 2012

From the above table, 48 (24.0%) respondents strongly agree that they feed better than they used to do while 114 (57.0%) respondents agree they feed better than they used to do then 13 (6.5%) respondents strongly disagree that feeding is better than it is used to be, 20 (10.0%) respondents disagree that feeding is better than it is used be and 5 (2.5%) respondents said they do not know whether feeding is better now or not. It can be concluded from this results that microcredit's have a positive impact on the respondents' ability to feed.

The following results were corroborated by Mrs. E, a union leader and loan beneficiary. According to her, the living condition of her and her family was very bad before joining the MFB. Since joining, things have become better. She explained that her plight was bad particularly because she was denied the needed education that would have given her the requisite skills and prepared her for the challenges of future life. This happened because according to her the parents divorced when she was still very young hence her mother who she was living with could provide for secondary education. But today I am doing well and able to support my family she stated. In her words; "with the profit from my business, I am able to care for my household. When my husband lost his job in 2006, the family depended solely on my income to survive. We did not feel it much. I was able to provide for feeding and the basic needs of my children. They are all doing well in school". She enjoined other poor women to subscribe to MFB's for loans as this could make them experience economic freedom.

Table 5.2.2: I am now able to buy my children's books and pay their fees

Variable	Frequency	Percent
Strongly Agree (SA)	35	17.5
Agree (A)	93	46.5
Strongly Disagree (SD)	29	14.5
Disagree (D)	24	12.0
None	19	9.5
Total	**200**	**100.0**

Source: Field Work, 2012

From the above table, 35 (17.5%) respondents strongly agree that they can now buy their children's books and pay their fees while 93 (46.5%) respondents agree they are now able to buy their children's books and pay their fees then 29 (14.5%) respondents strongly disagree that they can buy their children's text books and pay their fees, 24 (12.0%) respondents disagree that they can buy their children's books and pay their fees and 19 (9.5%) respondents said they cannot say whether their able to buy their children's books and pay their fees or not. These results shows that majority of the respondents/beneficiaries are able to provide for their children's educational needs.

For Mrs. A, initially it was thought to be impossible to send her child to school because according to her, she does not have the money to do so because her husband have abandoned her. After counseling and enlightening her that she can afford that it does not cost too much to send her child to school the woman yielded to the advice and the child was enrolled and he is now a 400 level undergraduate student. This case supports Sen's position that poverty is not just as a result of not enough money but lacking the capability to do act in certain way that one so desires. From this case also, it could be argued that enlightenment is important for the poor to realize their capability. Finally it supports the popular saying that "a poor man/woman is not a man without money, but a man without idea".

Table 5.2.3: I have been able to buy more equipment and household items

Variable	Frequency	Percent
Strongly Agree (SA)	31	15.5
Agree (A)	85	42.5
Strongly Disagree (SD)	35	17.5
Disagree (D)	31	15.5
None	18	9.0
Total	**200**	**100.0**

Source: Field Work, 2012

From the above table, 31 (15.5%) respondents strongly agree that they have been able to buy more equipment and household items while 85 (42.5%) respondents agree they have been able to buy more equipment and household items then 35 (17.5%) respondents strongly disagree that they are able to buy equipment and household items, 31 (15.5%) respondents disagree that they are able to buy equipment and household items and 18 (9.0%) respondents said they cannot say whether they were able to buy more equipment and household items or not.

Mrs. A, a union secretary with one of the MFB's, thanked the MFB for being a life saver for her and her family which hitherto went through trying and difficult moments. In her words, "It was a terrible experience, the situation was so serious that we were not able to feed our children very well…,we were forced into sleeping in the church for some time because we were not able to pay rent. Thank God today things are different for the better, we have been able to build our house and now have tenants". One observation from Mrs. A was that she was very industrious and hard working and have made good use of the loans she got to trying her hands in different businesses.

Table 5.2.4: I Now Wear Better Clothes than Before

Variable	Frequency	Percent
Strongly Agree (SA)	21	10.5
Agree (A)	89	44.5
Strongly Disagree (SD)	28	14.0
Disagree (D)	54	27.0
None	8	4.0
Total	**200**	**100.0**

Source: Field Work, 2012

From the above table, 21 (10.5%) respondents strongly agree that they wear better clothes now than before while 89 (44.5%) respondents agree they now wear better clothes than before then 28 (14.0%) respondents strongly disagree that they do wear better clothes now than before, 54 (27.0%) respondents disagree that they do wear better clothes now than before and 8 (4.0%) respondents said they cannot say whether they wear better clothes now or not.

Table 5.2.5: I am able to save some money now unlike before

Variable	Frequency	Percent
Strongly Agree (SA)	45	22.5
Agree (A)	112	56.0
Strongly Disagree (SD)	17	8.5
Disagree (D)	24	12.0
None	2	1.0
Total	**200**	**100.0**

Source: Field Work, 2012

From the above table, 45 (22.5%) respondents strongly agree that they are able to save some money now unlike before while 112 (56.0%) respondents agree they are able to save some money now unlike before then 17 (8.5%) respondents strongly disagree that they are able to save more money now like before, 24 (12.0%) respondents disagree that they are able to save more money now like before and 2 (1.0%) respondents said they cannot say whether they are able to save more money now like before or not.

Table 5.2.6: My business has grown/expanded than before

Variable	Frequency	Percent
Strongly Agree (SA)	47	23.5
Agree (A)	111	55.5
Strongly Disagree (SD)	22	11.0
Disagree (D)	14	7.0
None	6	3.0
Total	**200**	**100.0**

Source: Field Work, 2012

From the above table, 47 (23.5%) respondents strongly agree that their business has grown/expanded than before while 111 (55.5%) respondents agree that their business has grown/expanded than before then 22 (11.0%) respondents strongly disagree that their business had grown/expanded than before then 14 (7.0%) respondents disagree that their business had grown/expanded than before and 6 (3.0%) respondents said they cannot say whether their business had grown/expanded or not.

Discussant B. who is the leader of the Uwelu union of her MFB expressed happiness and noted that access to micro credits from MFB since 2002 have helped her food stuff business to expand tremendously and this she added have translated to more adequate support for her family.

Table 5.2.7: I can now treat myself better when sick than before

Variable	Frequency	Percent
Strongly Agree (SA)	23	11.5
Agree (A)	117	58.5
Strongly Disagree (SD)	13	6.5
Disagree (D)	37	18.5
None	10	5.0
Total	**200**	**100.0**

Source: Field Work, 2012

From the above table, 23 (11.5%) respondents strongly agree that they can now treat themselves better when sick than before while 117 (58.5%) respondents agree that they can now treat themselves better when sick than before then 13 (6.5%) respondents strongly disagree that they can now treat themselves better when sick than before, 37 (18.5%) respondents disagree that they have had any better treatment now than before and 10 (5.0%) respondents said that they cannot say whether they are able to treat themselves better now than before.

Mrs. O, who thanked the MFB for giving her the loan that enable her to start her tailoring business claims she realizes about 25,000 Naira (125 Euros) per month as profit from her business. She said that with this profit she can make adequate provisions for her children's basic needs as food, clothing, education and health care. In her words;"my condition has changed for the better, women should learn from my lessons. People are surprised about my progress in business. They had thought I won't be able to pay my children's school fees, but they are now disappointed". Finally, the case of Mrs. O reveals the stigma that poor people often face in Benin metropolis.

Table 5.2.8: My neighbors and friends have more respect for me now than before

Variable	Frequency	Percent
Strongly Agree (SA)	67	33.5
Agree (A)	90	45.0
Strongly Disagree (SD)	24	12.0
Disagree (D)	14	7.0
None	5	2.5
Total	**200**	**100.0**

Source: Field Work, 2012

From the above table, 67 (33.5%) respondents strongly agree that their neighbors and friends have respect for me now than before while 90 (45.0%) respondents agree that their neighbors and friends have respect for me now than before then 24 (12.0%) respondents strongly disagree that their neighbors and friends have more respect for me now than before, 14 (7.0%) respondents disagree that their neighbor and friends have more respect for me now than before and 5 (2.5%) respondents said that they cannot say whether their neighbors and friends have more respect for me now than before or not.

The case of Mrs. I was a woman who wanted to abandon the children and travel abroad for prostitution, upon counseling that she can live a meaningful life in Nigeria stayed back, and started getting loans from the MFB. Now, she is happy and no longer thinks of travelling abroad for prostitution and she is now able to train her children and one of the children is on scholarship with the microfinance NGO. The case of Mrs. I reveal the fact of how many people especially have been involved in forced migration abroad. Most of who end up being in prostitution and other forced labor.

5.3 Question three: The Policies, Regulatory and Supervisory Frameworks That Guide Microfinance Banks in Nigeria.

According to the CBN, 2011 revised microfinance policy framework for Nigeria, which was first launched in December 2005, the following are the policies, regulatory and supervisory frameworks guiding operations of MFB's in Nigeria:

- The CBN shall be responsible for the registration and licensing of MFB's in Nigeria, and such institutions must add "Microfinance Bank" to its name. And all such names are required to be registered with the Corporate Affairs Commission (CAC) in accordance with the Companies and Allied Matters Act (CAMA) 1990.
- All operators of MFB's are required to familiarize themselves with the revised regulatory and supervisory guidelines and comply with its provisions accordingly.
- Operators shall be required to obtain credit information from credit reference bureau to aid decision making and minimize risk.
- As a means of ensuring safety of depositors' funds and public confidence, MFB's shall qualify for the deposit insurance scheme of the National Deposit Insurance Corporation (NDIC).
- As a way of bridging the technical skills gap of the MFB's, the CBN have established the Microfinance Certification Program (MCP) to ensure the acquisition of requisite microfinance operational skills by staff and management of MFB's.
- The MFB's shall be required to make annual budgetary provision for staff development and capacity building programs.
- When established, the Microfinance Development Fund shall provide financial support for capacity building program for the MFB's on an on-going basis.
- Based on the importance of wholesale funds to MFI's which could enable them to expand their outreach, the CBN shall work out modalities for fostering linkages between MFB's/MFI's and DMB's/DFI's, specialized finance institutions and Donor Agencies to enable them source for wholesale funds for continuous lending to customers.
- MFB's shall disclose their sources of fund in accordance with the Money Laundering Prohibition Act 2004.

- The corporate governance principles shall be adhered to by all MFI's and the MFB's corporate governance shall be the direct responsibility of The Board of Directors by establishing strategic objectives, policies and procedures that would guide and direct the activities and the means to attain good corporate governance as well as setting up mechanisms for monitoring management's compliance.

There is no doubt that these frameworks are very germane to the success of MFB's in Nigeria. In fact the framework have led to the growth and expansion of MFB's in Nigeria as well as increased people's confidence in their operations. Mr. A, a general manager in one of the MFB's studied corroborated this fact. He puts it thus; "the government/CBN regulations gives them (MFB's) the ability to be competitive and also gives the clients increased confidence in the MFB because they are a registered and licensed organization by the government. They are no longer being seen as individual owners as it were before the MFB act/framework came into being when community banks where still operational". Also, Mrs. A, another top management staff in one of the MFB's Studied has this to say;" the role the government play is creating enabling environment for MFB's to operate and the CBN regulations have helped to create confidence on the MFB's. The fact that they are registered under the MFB policy increases this confidence and gives the MFB a good sense of focus because of the belief that someone is watching".

Based on the regulations the MFB's studied adopt two main methods in giving out loans to clients; the group method and individual method. The group method is usually targeted at the very poor and loan is given without collateral. The method entails a client joining a registered group/union recognized by the MFB and the group act as a security for the MFB. On request for loan, a successful member of the group is given a credit of N30, 000(thirty thousand Naira) which is approximately $200. Subsequently loan amount is increased after the clients have successful repay the previous one without default. It should be noted that over 80 percent of loans given out by the MFB's are by this method. The individual method is one were a client is given loan on an individual basis. The amount is usually bigger than the group method, but the individual must provide names of two verified guarantors who stand as surety for him/her. Common to both methods is the requirement that the client must open a savings account with the MFB. This is to enable them save and guarantee their commitment.

5.4 Question four: Problems/Challenges Hampering the Successful Implementation of the Microfinance Scheme.

From the field work results of this study, the following were the common views by respondents of the problems/challenges hampering the microfinance scheme in the study area:

- Too much demand requirements before loans are given
- Difficulties in getting guarantors by the clients
- Lack of trained and experienced microfinance experts
- High Interest Rate and Short repayment period
- Lack of care and attention by the MFB staff to the clients
- Communication problems between beneficiaries and MFB staff caused by poor literacy and multiple languages.
- The process and time of loan approval is too long
- The loan amount is too small to help clients expand their businesses
- High handedness of some leaders of MFB unions.
- Lack of direct support from the government e.g. failure to establish a microfinance development fund.
- Lack of adequate funds to meet the growing needs of the beneficiaries

5.5 Discussion of Results

While I agree with the fact that microfinance is a positive tool for poverty reduction as supported by the results of this study and other empirical literatures as cited in this research (for instance see Anyanwu, 2004, Yahaya, Osemene &Abdulkareem 2011), I will like to argue a bit by saying that despite these results of positive improvements in the life of MFB's beneficiaries, the fact still remains that millions of other people who are living in extreme poverty have not being touched or have not benefitted from the microfinance scheme. Hence they still remain in poverty (Morduch & Haley 2002).

The theoretical framework adopted in this study sees poverty not in the narrow sense of inadequacy of finance but in a holistic sense of other contributing factors depriving the poor of the basic abilities, 'functioning and capability' to live a meaningful life(Sen 1985,1999). Hence, wellbeing justice and development should be seen in terms of the people's capability to undertake any action and choose to become 'whom they want to be' (Robeyns 2005, p. 95). Consequently poverty can only be tackled effectively if these depriving factors are removed and the poor empowered to live a life he/she chooses to live. No doubt from the results of this study that microfinance has assisted many people in achieving this basic functioning and capability but many more others are still in the sidelines.

In other words, the results of the socio-demographic characteristics of the clients show a great dominance of the women over the men. This reinforces other previous studies that microfinance is very gender sensitive and has a specific bias for women. Some of the reasons for this includes firstly, the believe that women are soft hearted and pay back loans more than men and are more productive with microfinance by investing it in a trade or small business of which the profits is used to support the family. Secondly, the several societal discriminations against women make them more vulnerable to poverty than the men. For instance among the Benin ethnic group and others in Nigeria the women are deprived of inheritance. The practice of primogeniture makes it the automatic right of the first son to inherit the father's property and share amongst other male siblings were necessary, but the women are never considered. Considering the fact that a person can become rich via inheritance, the women have no possibility of acquiring this. In other words, the big commercial banks give loans majorly to the men because they are those that can provide the needed collaterals like houses, securities, and other valuables the women usually cannot provide.

Another important finding on the socio-demographic characteristics worthy of discussion here is that of education. Though a sizable proportion (30%) of the respondents have above NCE/OND which is an equivalent of a European A' Levels. The results still proved clearly right other research findings that the poor are people with little or no education. It also explains the fact that education is an instrument of 'equalizer' and empowerment that help prepare people for the challenges of future life and consequently liberate and lift them out of poverty. This is not to say that all poorly educated people are living in poverty, but the majority of the poor are uneducated. This supports the vicious circle theory of poverty which opines that the circumstance of the poor contribute to maintain them in poverty (Haralambus & Heald 1980). Hence, it can conveniently be inferred that one plausible way of tackling the menace of poverty is to provide quality education to the poor as this will enable them to be equipped with adequate knowledge and skills and by implication the empowerment and capability to live a good life (see Sen 1988, 1999) and break off the vicious circle of poverty.

Results from the second question which is the impact of microfinance on the living standard and wellbeing of beneficiaries showed a positive result on all the groups of questions asked. For instance majority of respondents agreed that compared to before taking the loans they can feed better now, buy their children's books and pay school fees, able to save more money and expand business and threat themselves better when sick. Most of the successful beneficiaries have been successful owing to their great entrepreneur skills and great drive to achieve- traits rare in many poor people who are mostly disillusioned and frustrated by their debacle situation.

For the purpose of clarity, it should be noted that the period of comparism done here is an average of two years given the fact that majority of the clients (see table 5.1.7)have borrowed more than two times from the MFB's. The period of repayment after the first loan is usually 8 months after which application is sent for the second loan which takes some months to approve, consequently a client that have borrowed more than twice must have been accessing the loan for a period of not less than 2 years. The years are longer for the union leaders interviewed most of whom have been accessing credits for more than five years. Despite the positive impact of the loans as agreed by these clients it is not enough to over celebrate because the level of poverty is very endemic in the country and specifically in the study area. This is exacerbated by the problem of poor outreach of the MFB's where millions of extreme poor have not been reached. According to Morduch & Harley (2002) microfinance has not been able to sufficiently penetrate the poorer strata of the society. Several other studies corroborate this, so also does macro data on poverty which revealed an alarming increase of the scourge. For instance see (Bamisile 2005, Charles & Hamid 2005, Lafourde Et al 2005, Tables 2.3.1 & 2.3.2).

The third question is the policies, regulatory and supervisory frameworks which guide micro-finance banks in Nigeria. The launching of microfinance policy framework first in December 2005 and its subsequent review in 2011 have led to tremendous growth of the microfinance sector, and have equally led to increase clients and public confidence in microfinance operations in Nigeria. Although registered microfinance institutions have increased to over 900, the out-reach and contribution to GDP is still very poor given the fact that about 70% of the people live in poverty. In 2005, the share of micro credit as a percentage of total credit was 0.9%, while the sector contributed a meager 0.2 Percent of the GDP (Bamisile 2006). The non implementation of some of the microfinance policies like the establishment of microfinance development fund has contributed to increase the problem of poor clients' outreach. The policy framework has not also been able to mitigate the problem of over concentration of the microfinance institutions in the urban areas. Given the fact that majority of Nigeria's poor reside in the rural areas, resolving this problem will go a long way in increasing access to finance for the poor.

The fourth question which is the general constraints hampering the successful implementation of the micro-finance scheme highlighted some of the problems bedeviling the sector, some of which have already been discussed. The problem of high interest rate is one that must be looked into. The present rate of between 30% and over40 % charged as interest by MFB's in Nigeria is too high and unsustainable. A lot of other literatures and empirical findings also support this. Consequently, if microfinance is to achieve its goal of poverty reduction in Nigeria, this is one problem that must be addressed by all relevant stake holders so as to bring more benefits to the poor clients.

Mohammed Yunus, the founder of Gramaen Bank, Bangladesh and a Noble Peace Prize Winner in microfinance also corroborates the problem of high interest rate charged by MFB's in Nigeria. Speaking at an international conference on microfinance held at Lagos, Nigeria in 2011 he focused on microfinance experience in Bangladesh and 'took a swipe' at the Central Banks of most nations of the world including Nigeria that they do not know or understand the principles of microfinance banking. He added that the high rate of interest charged in Nigeria defeats the purpose of microfinance and does not serve the interest of the poor hence he opined that what is being practice in Nigeria is 'not microfinance banking, but micro commercial bank' (http://microfinanceafrica.net/tag/microfinance-in-nigeria). The problems of poor infrastructural base and lack of basic amenities like water, electricity has contributed to increase the cost of doing business and ultimately the profits of the clients who are micro-entrepreneurs (Yahaya, Osemene & Abdulraheem 2011).For instance, buying of petrol/diesel in Nigeria by small business owners to fuel a power generating set because of epileptic supply of electricity increases cost and ultimately profit.

CHAPTER SIX

Recommendation and Conclusion

6.1 Recommendations

Findings from this study have revealed lots of problems bedeviling the continuous success of the microfinance sector in Benin Metropolis in particular and Nigeria at large. The following recommendations are therefore put forward to help tackle these problems and make microfinance more accessible and beneficial to the poor in Benin Metropolis and Nigeria in general.

- The high interest rates charged by microfinance which is 15% over the cost of borrowing from the big commercial banks should be reduced to not more than 5% of cost of borrowing so as to reduce the burden on the clients.
- The government, specifically the CBN should collaborate with the MFB's in the area of manpower training so as to increase the numbers of professionals or experts in the sector.
- The loan approval process of the MFB's should be faster as to reduce the period of loan approval and ensure quick access of credits to the clients.
- The present threshold amount of N30, 000(thirty thousand Naira) approximately $200 should be increased to N60, 000 (sixty thousand Naira) $400 so as to give the clients/borrowers more capital for their businesses.
- The period of loan repayment should be extended beyond the present 6 to 8 months to between 15 to 18 months.
- The process of setting up of the planned microfinance development fund by the government should be expedited as this would help provide more liquidity for the microfinance banks and therefore increase their outreach to other numerous poor clients.
- The CBN and all other necessary agencies of government should work vigorously to ensure that more MFB's are located in the rural areas. This is necessary because majority of the poor in Nigeria reside in the rural areas and this will it easier for them to access needed credits.
- The provision of basic infrastructures and amenities should be vigorously pursued by the government. Also the problem of corruption which is ubiquitous in Nigeria and that of good governance should be effectively and urgently tackled because the success or

failure of the microfinance scheme or any other poverty reduction strategy rest very much on these.

6.2 Conclusion

This study investigated the role of micro finance in poverty reduction in Nigeria. The study particularly focused on the capacity of the micro finance scheme beneficiaries to successfully navigate their way out of the vicious circle of poverty. The survey design was adopted. The questionnaire was administered to respondents in addiction to one session of focus group discussion (FGD) which was organized for MFB's beneficiaries. In dept interview was organized for management officers of the micro finance institutions. And I participation in one union meeting of 40 members were some useful observations were noted. The result of the analysis reveals a lot of progress and Positive outcome for the beneficiaries/clients of MFB's in Benin Metropolis who agreed that microfinance have helped lift them out of poverty. This greatly supports the results of similar studies that have reported favorable and better living standards for MFB's Beneficiaries. However, this positive outcome does not mean that the microfinance framework is problem free. In fact, the prospects of micro finance as a poverty reduction tool is being threatened by poor outreach to clients especially those in the rural areas who do not have access to these credits. A problem caused by unbiased location of MFB's, inadequate fund and harsh fiscal policy on the part of micro finance institutions. Notwithstanding the problems fore stated militating against micro finance scheme as poverty reduction strategy, the prospects of helping to fight the hydra headed endemic poverty in Nigeria via micro credits is still a viable and sustainable option.

However, given the fact that the problem of poverty is multidimensional and ubiquitous in Nigeria and based on the challenges militating against the microfinance sector it becomes imperative to opine that achieving wide scale poverty reduction via microfinance alone is quite uncertain in the nearest future. Hence more research still needs to be done about the impact of microfinance especially on how to increase its outreach on a wide scale. Similarly, a juxtaposition of the successes of microfinance in alleviating poverty with the relevant macro data on poverty reveals that the success of microfinance is just a 'pinch of salt' that is very little compared to the number of people living in poverty. For instance the percentage of Nigerians living in poverty as at 2010 was 69.0% of the population that is 112 million people (NBS, 2012).

Similarly, State of Microcredit Summit Campaign Report 2012 reveals that 12,692,579 people in Sub-Saharan Africa are being served by microfinance. For instance if all of these people were Nigerians of which they are not, it will just be about 12% outreach of the total number of poor. Consequent upon the above it becomes clear that microfinance alone cannot reduce poverty absolutely in Nigeria. Hence to achieve more success in this regards some other core factors like unemployment, corruption, non diversification of the economy, income inequality and poor education and infrastructural base which are key contributors to the increase rate of poverty in Nigeria (Ucha, 2010) needs to be adequately addressed because they are core factors that deprives the poor of the needed capabilities to live a life of 'adequate well being' (Sen 1988; 1993).

REFERENCES

Aigbokhan, B. E. (2008). *Growth, inequality and poverty in Nigeria.* Prepared for United Nations Economic Commission for Africa (UNECA). Addis Ababa, Ethiopia.

Akanji, O. O. (2002). Microfinance as a strategy for poverty reduction. *CBN economic and Financial Review*, *39*(4), 18-28.

Akindola, R. B. (2009). Towards a Definition of Poverty Poor People's Perspectives and Implications for Poverty Reduction. *Journal of Developing Societies*, *25*(2), 121-150.

Anyanwu, C. M. (2004, November). Microfinance institutions in Nigeria: policy, practice and potentials. In *G24 Workshop on Constraints to Growth in Sub-Saharan Africa* (pp.29- 30).

Bamisile, A.S. (2006) Developing a Long Term Sustainable Microfinance Sector in Nigeria: The Way Forward. Washington,D.C., USA, October 23 – 27

CBN,(2005). *Microfinance Policy Framework For Nigeria.* Abuja: CBN.

CBN,(2011). *Revised Microfinance Policy Framework For Nigeria.* Abuja: CBN.

Chambers, R. (1994). "The origins and practice of PRA." *World Development* ***22(7)***.

Chambers, R. (1997). *Whose Reality Counts? Putting the First Last.* London: Intermediate Technology Publications.

Charles, J. A. & Hamed, A. B. (2005).Influence of Loan Disbursement by Microfinance and Non Microfinance Institutions on Poverty Alleviation in Nigeria. *Business and Management Sciences 1(4) 198-205*

Chinsinga, B. (2003). The participatory development approach under a microscope: the case of the poverty alleviation programme in Malawi. *Journal of social development in Africa*,*18*(1), 129-144.

Chukwuma Dim, C. (2013) Poverty Trap in Nigeria; a Multidimensional perspective. Retrieved 19/02/2013fromhttp://werdiscussion.worldeconomicsassociation.org/wp/content/uploads/Poverty-Trap-in-Nigeria-a-multidimensional-perspective.pd

Coudouel, A., Hentschel, J. S., & Wodon, Q. T. (2002). Poverty measurement and analysis. *A Sourcebook for poverty reduction strategies*, *1*, 1260.

Devas, N. (2004). *Urban Governance, Voice and Poverty in the Developing World.* James & James/Earthscan.

Dodson, L. and Schmalzbauer, L. (2005), Poor Mothers and Habits of Hiding: Participatory methods in Poverty Research. Journal of Marriage and Family, 67: 949–959. doi: 10.1111/ j.1741-3737.2005.00186.x

Dobra, A. (2011). Microfinance: Champion in Poverty Alleviation and Failure in Female Empowerment. *Internationale Politik und Gesellschaft , 3,(3) 134-144.*

Ehigiamusoe, G. (2011). *Issues in Microfinance: Enhancing Financial Inclusion.* Benin: Mindex Publishing Co. Ltd.

Enebeli, Uzor (2009). Positioning Agriculture for Nigeria's Economic Development. *Zenith Economic Quarterly 4, 1* January 2009

FRN (2001). National Poverty Eradication Program. Abuja: FRN

Haralambus, M. & Heald, R. (1980). Sociology: Themes and Perspectives. Oxford: Oxford University Press.

Hulme, D., & McKay, A. (2005). Identifying and measuring chronic poverty: Beyond monetary measures. *Chronic Poverty Research Centre Working Paper*, (30).

Ikechukwu, A. (2012). Microfinance Banking in Nigeria: Problems and Prospects. *International Journal of Finance and Accounting,* 1(5): 106-111.

Iyoha, M.A.(2005).*When will Africa's Sleeping Giant Awake*? Inaugural lecture series; University of Benin, May 19, 2005.

Kelley, K., Clark, B., Brown, V., & Sitzia, J. (2003). Good practice in the conduct and reporting of survey research. *International Journal for Quality in Health Care*, *15*(3), 261-266.

Jick, T. D. (1979). Mixing qualitative and quantitative methods: Triangulation in action. *Administrative science quarterly*, *24*(4), 602-611.

Jitsuchon, S. (2001). What is Poverty and How to Measure it. *TDRI Quarterly Review 7-11*

Laderchi, C. R. (2000). *The monetary approach to poverty: a survey of concepts and methods*. Queen Elizabeth House.

Laderchi, C. R., Saith, R., & Stewart, F. (2003). Does it matter that we do not agree on the definition of poverty? A comparison of four approaches. *Oxford Development Studies*, *31*(3), 243-274.

Lafourcade, A. L., Isern, J., Mwangi, P., & Brown, M. (2005). Overview of the outreach and financial performance of microfinance institutions in Africa. *Microfinance InformationeX-change,Washington,DC.http://www.mixmarket.org/medialibrary/mixmarket/Africa_ Data_Study. pdf.*

LAPO, (2009). Annual Report & Accounts 2009.Benin City: Lapo.

Maes, J. P., & Reed, L. R. (2012). State of the Microcredit Summit Campaign Report 2012.*Microcredit Summit Campaign, Washington, DC.*

Maxwell, S. (2009). T*he meaning and measurement of poverty*. Retrieved 18/02/2013 from http://dspace.cigilibrary.org/jspui/handle/123456789/22749

Midgley, J. (2008). Microenterprise, global poverty and social development. *International Social Work*, *51*(4), 467-479.

Montgomery, H. and Weiss, J. (2005). "Great Expectations: Microfinance and Poverty Reduction in Asia and Latin America", *ADB Institute Research Paper Series, No. 63*.

Morduch, J., & Haley, B. (2002). Analysis of the effects of microfinance on poverty reduction. *New York: NYU Wagner Working Paper*, (1014).

NBS(2005).*Nigeria Poverty Profile 2004*.Abuja: NBS

NBS(2012).*Nigeria Poverty Profile 2010*.Abuja: NBS.

Nussbaum, M. (2003). Capabilities as fundamental entitlements: Sen and social justice. *Feminist economics*, *9*(2-3), 33-59.

O'Boyle, J. E.(1999).Toward an Improved Definition of Poverty. *The Review of Social Economy, 9, 1-20.*

Obadan, M. I. (2002).Poverty Reduction in Nigeria: The way forward. *CBN Economic and Financial Review, 39(4), 29-59*

Odusola, A.F.(1997).Poverty in Nigeria: An Eclectic Appraisal. *In Poverty Alleviation in Nigeria: Selected Papers for The 1997 Annual Conference.* Ibadan: Pat Mag Press Ltd.

Ogwumike, F. O. (2002). An appraisal of poverty reduction strategies in Nigeria. *CBN Economic and Financial Review*, *39*(4), 1-17.

Okpi, A. (2012, April 8).66 million Nigerians lack access to potable water – WHO/UNICEF. *Punch.* Retrieved 26/08/2012 from http://www.punchng.com/news/66-million-nigerians-lack-access-to-potable-water-whounicef/

Omotola, J. S. (2008). Combating poverty for sustainable human development in Nigeria: The continuing struggle. *Journal of poverty*, *12*(4), 496-517.

Oshewolo, S. (2010). Galloping poverty in Nigeria: an appraisal of the government's interventionist policies. *Journal of Sustainable Development in Africa*, *12*(6), 264-274.

Punch, Keith (2005).*Introduction to Social Research: Quantitative and Qualitative Approaches.* London: Sage Publications.

Ravallion, M. (2003). The debate on globalization, poverty and inequality: why measurement matters. *International Affairs*, *79*(4), 739-753.

Ringen, S. (2009). Poverty—The Rowntree Project revisited. *Paper delivered at the Kennedy School of Government, Harvard University. Retrieved June*, *1*, 2009.

Robeyns, Ingrid (2011)."The Capability Approach", *The Stanford Encyclopedia of Philosophy (Summer 2011 Edition)*, Edward N. Zalta (ed.) retrieved 21/02/2012 from; http://plato.stanford.edu/archives/sum2011/entries/capability-approach/

Robeyns, I. (2005). The capability approach: a theoretical survey. *Journal of human development*, *6*(1), 93-117.

Rosenfeld, J. (2010). 'The meaning of poverty'and contemporary quantitative poverty research1. *The British Journal of Sociology*, *61*, 103-110.

Sen, A. (1983). Poor, relatively speaking. *Oxford economic papers*, *35*(2), 153-169.

Sen, A. (1984). The living standard. *Oxford Economic Papers*, 74-90.

Sen, A. (1985). A sociological approach to the measurement of poverty: a reply to Professor Peter Townsend. *Oxford Economic Papers*, 669-676.

Sen, A. (1985b). Well-being, agency and freedom: the Dewey lectures 1984. *The Journal of Philosophy*, 169-221.

Sen, A. (1988). The concept of development. *Handbook of development economics*, *1*, 9-26.

Sen, A. (1993). Capability and well-being. *The quality of life*, *1*(9), 30-54.

Sen, A. (1999). *Development as freedom*. Oxford University Press.

Spicker, P. (1999). Definitions of poverty: eleven clusters of meaning. *The international glossary on poverty. London: Zed Books*, 150-62.

Subair, G. (2012, February 13). Nigeria's poverty level rises, hits 71.5%.Nigerian Tribune. Retrieved 26/08/2012 from http://tribune.com.ng/index.php/front-page-news/35947-nigerias-poverty-level-rises-hits-715-sokoto-niger-top-list-of-poorest-states.

Tell (2009, October 5). The Making of a Failed State. 40, 15-16.

The Nation (2012, August 29). UNDP rues rising poverty, unemployment in Nigeria. TheNation. Retrieved 29/08/2012 from http://www.thenationonlineng.net/2011/news-update/59495-undp-rues-rising-poverty-unemployment-in-nigeria.html

Townsend, P. (2010). The Meaning of Poverty. *The British journal of sociology*, *61*(s1), 85-102.

Tseng, C. C. (2011). *Microfinance and Amartya Sen's capability approach* (Doctoral dissertation, University of Birmingham).

Ucha, C. (2010). Poverty in Nigeria: Some dimensions and contributing factors. *Global Majority E-Journal*, *1*(1), 46-56.

Udeh, J. (2000). *Petroleum Revenue Mgt. the Nigerian perspective.* Paper presented at the World Bank/IFC Petroleum Revenue Mgt Workshop, Washington D.C, USA Oct 23-24 2000.

Ugiagbe, E.O (2012) *Women and Poverty Alleviation: A Study of the Impacts of Micro-Credits Schemes on Female Beneficiaries in South Senatorial District of Edo State*. (Phd Thesis).Ambrose Alli University, Ekpoma, Nigeria

UNDP (1997). Human Development Report, United Nations Development Programme(UNDP). Oxford University Press, New York.

Uniamikogbo, S.O. (1997).Poverty Alleviation Under Structural Adjustment Program: A Policy Framework. *In Poverty Alleviation in Nigeria: Selected Papers for The 1997 Annual Conference*. Ibadan: Pat Mag Press Ltd.

UNICEF (2007). *A community based violence against refugees, returnees and internally displaced persons:* Guidelines for prevention and response, Geneva, United Nations High Commissioner for Refugees.

Weisfeld-Adams, E. & Andrzejewski, A.(2008). Hunger & Poverty: Definition and Distinctions. T*he Hunger Project, New York 1-5*

WHO(2012).*Poverty.* Retrieved 22/11/2012 from http://www.who.int/topics/poverty/en/retrieved

World Bank (2000). World development report 2000/2001; Attacking poverty, the World Bank Group, Oxford University Press, New York.

Yahaya, K. A., & Osemene, O. F. (2011). Effectiveness of Microfinance Banks in Alleviating Poverty in Kwara State Nigeria. *Global Journal of Management And Business Research*, *11*(4) 13-20.

Yin, Robert (1984). Case Study Research: Design and Methods. Thousand Oaks, California: Sage Publications.

APPENDIX ONE Questionnaire Guide December, 2012.

Dear Sir/Madam,

I am a Master's Degree Student and I am Carrying out a Research on:
MICRO FINANCE & POVERTY REDUCTION IN NIGERIA: A STUDY OF SELECTED MICRO-FINANCE INSTITUTIONS IN BENIN METROPOLIS, SOUTH SOUTH OF NIGERIA.

The research is for the partial fulfillment of the requirements for the award of Master's of Arts (MA) in Social Science by the Philosophical Faculty of Albert-Ludwigs – University, Freiburg (Germany) and Facultad Latinoamericana de ciencias sociales (FLACSO), Buenos Aires, (Argentina).

I wish to obtain some information from you to enable me carry out the research successfully.

I assure you that any information received from you will be used strictly for academic purpose only and treated confidentially.

Thanks for your anticipated cooperation.

Yours sincerely,

Uyi Benjamin Edegbe

QUESTIONNAIRE/INTERVIEW GUIDE FOR MICRO-FINANCE LOANS BENEFICIARIES

SECTION A:

Socio-Demographic Data/Respondents Profile

1. What is your age next-birthday?
   - Below 20 years [ ]
   - 21-40 years [ ]
   - 41-60 years [ ]
   - Above 60 years [ ]
2. Sex
   - Male [ ]
   - Female [ ]
3. Water is your marital status?
   - Single [ ]
   - Married [ ]
   - Separated [ ]
   - Widowed [ ]
4. What is your highest level of education?
   - None [ ]
   - Primary School Leaving certificate [ ]
   - Junior Secondary [ ]
   - Senior Secondary/NECO/GCE [ ]
   - National Diploma/NCE [ ]
   - HND/First Degree [ ]
   - Masters/Ph.D. [ ]
5. What is your religion?
   - Christianity [ ]
   - Islam [ ]
   - Others [ ]
6. Which work do you do for a living?
   - Trading/Business [ ]
   - Civil service work [ ]
   - Teaching
   - Others (Please state) ______________________________
7. What is your ethnic group? ______________________________
8. How many times have you borrowed from Micro-Finance Institutions(s)
   - Once [ ]
   - Twice [ ]
   - More Than Twice [ ]

9. How many of your children are still in school?

None [ ]
1-3 [ ]
Above 4 [ ]

SECTION B:

Respondents' Perception of Micro-Finance Institutions Services

1. What is your view about the interest rate charged by Micro-Finance Institutions
   Low [ ]
   Moderate [ ]
   High [ ]
   Too High [ ]
2. Do Micro-Finance Institutions give you loans on time when you apply?
   Yes [ ]
   Sometimes [ ]
   Too much delay [ ]
   Not at all [ ]
3. Are Micro-Finance Institutions' workers friendly with clients?
   Yes [ ]
   No [ ]
   Can't say [ ]
   No comment [ ]
4. Do Micro-Finance Institution discriminate when giving loans to applicants?
   Yes [ ]
   No [ ]
   Can't say [ ]
5. Is the repayment period of Micro-finance Institutions okay by you?
   Yes [ ]
   No [ ]
   Not at all [ ]
6. Do Micro-Finance Institutions show interest in your business?
   Yes [ ]
   No [ ]
7. It "Yes", how do they show interest? (Explain)
   (a) ______________________________
   (b) ______________________
   (c) ______________________________
8. If "No", how do you know they do not show interest? (Explain)
   (a) ______________________________
   (b) ______________________________
   (c) ______________________________

9. What is your view about the amount of loans Micro-Finance Institutions give?
   Satisfactory [ ]
   Not Enough [ ]
   Too small [ ]

SECTION C

Assessment of Impacts of Micro-Finance Institutions on Beneficiaries

Assessment of Impact of Micro-Finance Institutions on Beneficiaries				
Since I started borrowing from Micro-Finance Institution	**SA**	**A**	**SD**	**D**
I feed better than I used to do				
I am now able to buy my children's books and pay their fees				
I have now been able to buy more equipments and household items				
I now wear better clothes than before				
I am able to save some money now unlike before				
My business has grown/expanded than before				
I can now treat myself better when sick than before				
My neighbours and friends have more respect for me now than before				

SECTION D

What are the constraints customers faces when trying to borrowing money from micro-Finance Institutions?

1. ______________________________
2. ______________________________
3. ______________________________

SECTION E

How service of Micro-Finance Institutions be improved to benefit borrowers? (Please list your view)

1. ______________________________
2. ______________________________
3. ______________________________
4. ______________________________

Thank you

Appendix 2 Interview Schedule for Managers/Directors of Micro Credit Outfits

(1) **Organization Background:** Why was your outfit floated and join the train of poverty reduction organization? How long have your organizations been in business? Is your organization privately owned, public limited company or jointly own as family business? Probe further in responses to these questions.

(2) **Organization Background Information:** What is the staff strength and operational structure of your organization? What are the values and philosophies of your organization? What are the group and organizational dynamics of your outfits? How many branches outlets do you have? Probe further.

(3) **Group Activities:** What is the nature of the organizational organogram and operations of your outfit? How and who relate with the female beneficiaries in your outfit? What is the exact number or estimate of the female beneficiaries of your outfit? Is your organization gendered balanced or biased? How and on what ground do you give out credit facilities? What is the nature of the facilities – cash or services or goods? How many female groups are registered with your organization? What are the collaterals, terms and conditions of the loans and repayment? Probe further.

(4) **Finance:** How and where do you source for finance for your organization? Where do you get your finances from: locally, internationally? As AID, borrowing, selling bonds etc?

(5) **Government and Fiscal Policies:** What is the role of government in your organization? What is the impact of various fiscal policies, regulations and financial climate on your organizational goals and aspirations? Explain whether the global economic meltdown has affected your organizational goals and aspirations or not?

(6) What are the difficulties that you experience in achieving the aims and objectives of your organization? How have your been coping with these challenges? Do you agree to the notion that micro finance is a veritable tool for poverty alleviation in Nigeria? What are your reservations about your clients/groups doing business with your organization?

(7) Why do you persist and persevere as leading micro finance outfit? What keeps you going If given a second chance will you remain in this business or venture into something else? Any recommendations to the government? Researchers? International organizations?

Appendix 3 Focus Group Discussion Guide for Leaders of Registered Unions of Micro Finance Banks

- **Bio-data information of unions:** When was your union formed? How many members have your union? What are the requirements for registration of a union with the micro credit organization?
- **Membership:** What are the prerequisites for membership of the union? What is the organizational structure and the roles of the group leaders?
- What are the modalities for taking a loan and repayment to the micro credit organizations by the unions and the members?
- What are the challenges, problems or constraints your union face or still facing? What are the natures of these constraints or challenges?
- **Government:** What are the roles you think government should play in the life of the people? What area will you want government to intervene in the affairs of your union?
- **Loan:** How much can you borrow as a union from micro credit organizations? What are the collaterals and modalities of loan repayment? What will you do to a member who defaults in payment of loan? What other ways do your union assist its members? – training, monitoring, counselling etc.
- What are your reservations about micro finance and micro credit organizations? How do you assess your members' performance in the past three years as members of this union? If given second time, will you join the union and/or utilise micro credit facilities? What are the way forward in your opinion on the problem facing female beneficiaries and micro credit schemes in Nigeria?

Characteristics Name Optimal	**1**	**2**	**3**	**4**	**5**	**6**	**7**	**8**	**9**	**10**
Actual age										
Sex										
Marital status										
Highest level of education										
Occupation/business										
Monthly income										
Ethnic background										

Please fill this form before the commencement of the discussion. Emphasize the fact that confidentiality is assured.

Appendix 4 List of Registered Micro Finance Banks in Benin City

S/N	ABC MFB	Mission Road, Okada, Ovia North-East L.G.A. and 178, Upper Siluko Road, Benin City.
1	Circular MFB	66, First East Circular Road, Benin City.
2	Cubic MFB	1, Agbado Street, Benin City
3	Cutting Edge MFB	58, Oregbani, Ramat Park.
4	Ehor MFB	7, Royal Street, P.O. Box 6, Ehor Uhunmwode L.G.A., 2nd Circular Road, Benin City.
5	Ighomo MFB	7, Akpakpava Road, Benin City
6	Ivie MFB	108, Sapele Road, Benin City
7	UFT MFB	6, S & T Road, Uselu, Benin
8	Okuta MFB	612, Efianagi Iyayi Road, Egva Land Uhumwode L.G.A.
9	Prosperity MFB	Jeremiah 17B Place 1, Siluko Benin City
10	Trustfund MFB	6, Adesuwa Road, G.R.A., Benin City
11	Edo MFB	248, Ugbowo-Lagos Road, Egor L.G.A.
12	Lofty Heights MFB	102, Edo Textile Mill Road, Benin City.
13	Astrick MFB	M.M. Way, Benin City.
14	PM Bank MFB	Siluko Road, Benin City.
15	Isi MFB	M.M. Way, Benin City.
16	Alaghodaro MCB	1st Circular Road, Benin City.
17	LAPO MFB	Dawson Road and S & T Road Uselu, Benin City.
18	EDOMO MFB	James Watt Street, Benin City & Upper Siluko Road, Benin City.
19	Union Loans Ltd	New Lagos Road, Benin City.
20	Nova Micro Finance Ltd	Upper Sakponba Road, Benin City.
21	Trustfund Ltd	Plot 78, Upper Erumwunse Street, Benin City.
22	Akugbe Cooperative	Ikpoba Hill, Benin City.

	MFB	
23	Nagbama Micro Finance	Iriri Benin City
24	Akugbe Community MFB	Upper Uwelu, Benin City.
25	Progressive MFB	M.M. Way, Benin City.